Stories of
DIVINE
HEALING

DESTINY IMAGE BOOKS BY RANDY CLARK

Baptized in the Holy Spirit

Power to Heal

The Essential Guide to the Power of the Holy Spirit (with Bill Johnson)

God Can Use Little Ole Me

Power/Holiness/Evangelism

Authority to Heal

Stories of
DIVINE
HEALING

SUPERNATURAL TESTIMONIES

that IGNITE FAITH *for*

Your Healing

Randy Clark

DESTINY IMAGE® PUBLISHERS, INC.

P.O. Box 310, Shippensburg, PA 17257-0310

"Promoting Inspired Lives."

This book and all other Destiny Image and Destiny Image Fiction books are available at Christian bookstores and distributors worldwide.

Cover design by Eileen Rockwell

Interior design by Terry Clifton

For more information on foreign distributors, call 717-532-3040.

Reach us on the Internet: www.destinyimage.com.

ISBN 13 TP: 978-0-7684-1636-7

ISBN 13 eBook: 978-0-7684-1635-0

ISBN 13 HC: 978-0-7684-1634-3

ISBN 13 LP: 978-0-7684-1637-4

For Worldwide Distribution, Printed in the U.S.A.

1 2 3 4 5 6 7 8 / 22 21 20 19 18

And when Jesus went out He saw a great multitude;
and He was moved with compassion
for them, and healed their sick.
—MATTHEW 14:14 NKJV

CONTENTS

INTRODUCTION *by Bill Johnson*
1

THE SUPERNATURAL POWER OF A TESTIMONY
7

CANCER
15

CIRCULATORY SYSTEM
31

DELIVERANCE
41

DIGESTIVE SYSTEM
83

ENDOCRINE SYSTEM
97

IMMUNE SYSTEM
113

INTEGUMENTARY SYSTEM
125

MARRIAGE AND FAMILY
131

MUSCULAR SYSTEM
137

NERVOUS SYSTEM
171

REPRODUCTIVE SYSTEM
217

RESPIRATORY SYSTEM
223

SKELETAL SYSTEM
231

URINARY SYSTEM
261

INDEX
266

INTRODUCTION

By Bill Johnson

I remember as a young pastor having an unusual experience while reading the book of Revelation. It happened when I came upon the verse, "the testimony of Jesus in the Spirit of prophecy" (see Rev. 19:10). I could feel the presence of God on that verse. I know He blesses the entire Bible, but this was different. It's really hard to explain, but I felt drawn to it, longing to understand it better. Looking back, it seemed to be an assignment. In that moment, I stopped reading and asked the Lord to show me what it meant. Little did I know that this simple one-sentence prayer would have such a profound effect on the rest of my life, but it did. That was about thirty-five years ago.

A few hours or so later a member of our church family stopped by to tell me a story. He was in somewhat of a hurry, so he stood in the doorway. He began to explain how God had healed his marriage, and he was so grateful. When he turned to leave, he stopped, and turning back around, he said, "You are free to share this story with anyone you want." I knew immediately that this moment was connected to the prayer I had prayed earlier. God's presence becomes manifest when He breathes upon someone's words. My friend had shared a testimony with me that I could share (prophesy) with others.

I began to ponder what had just happened, and came to this understanding. First, *the testimony of Jesus* is a spoken or written record of anything that God has done. Second, *the spirit of prophecy* is the anointing for the prophetic. Third, *prophecy* either foretells the future or changes the present. It started to make sense to me. Anytime we give a testimony of what God has done, it releases the anointing to change present circumstances through the reoccurrence of the spoken miracle.

Several years ago, Randy Clark sent this quote to me from Charles Spurgeon that showed me he had this same understanding:

> When people hear about what God used to do, one of the things they say is: "Oh, that was a very long while ago."... I thought it was God that did it. Has God changed? Is he not an immutable God, the same yesterday, today and forever? Does not that furnish an argument to prove that what God has done at one time he can do at another? Nay, I think I may push it a little further and say **what he has done once is a prophecy of what he intends to do again ....Whatever God has done...is to be looked upon as a precedent** .... [Let us] with earnestness seek that God would restore to us the faith of the men of old, that we may richly enjoy his grace as in the days of old.[1] (Emphasis mine).

Spurgeon was one of the most important pastors in church history. And he understood this concept that has tragically been forgotten or pushed aside until recent days. Interestingly, Spurgeon uses the word *precedent*. In our court systems, they frequently research the court records to find a similar case to the one being tried. They do this to see what the courts decided before. It's called *legal precedent*. Once a legal

---

1   http://www.spurgeon.org/sermons/0263.htm

precedent has been found, the case being tried becomes an open-and-shut case.

Every time we hear a testimony of what God has done, we are looking at a legal precedent. God has already revealed His will, His nature and His promises through the miracle spoken of. And since He is the same yesterday, today, and forever, *and* He is no respecter of persons, we have the grounds to contend for our own breakthrough revealed through the testimony. I like to think of all testimonies as invitations by God for us to come to know Him in the way revealed in the story.

The Journey

A number of years after my original question and experience with the testimony, I discovered more of what God intended for me in the beginning of this story. I began to notice that the weightiness of God's presence was sometimes released during a testimony. I would then experiment with the concept by looking for people who had the same condition that was healed in the testimony. I was shocked to find that often people would be healed after the testimony was given, especially if we took a few minutes to give instruction. Interestingly, I remember many testimonies while growing up in church, and yet I don't ever remember anyone getting healed. It seems that simply understanding how God moves through the testimony and then putting faith into an action was all that was needed to complete the equation. While there are many, many stories to support this concept, I'll share one for illustration's sake. A little three-year-old boy was healed of clubfeet on the coast of Northern California. The following Sunday I shared the testimony with our church family. Unknown to me, a woman visiting our church from another state had a little girl in our nursery who was almost two years old. Her feet turned inward so severely that she would trip over them when she tried to run. The mother heard the story of God healing the clubfeet, and then, hearing the concept of a testimony being a prophecy, she said in her heart, "I'll take that for my daughter." When she picked up her little girl from our child care services, her feet were already straight. No one had prayed for her.

These kinds of stories have been piling up for years. What we've noticed in this journey is MANY more breakthroughs happen when people understand the truth about a testimony being prophetic. Secondly, once the testimony is given, people need to act. The minimum is that they need to examine themselves to see what has happened. Certainly, it could be said that some are healed and don't know it until they get home. But typically, an action of some sort is needed at the moment the story is heard.

The power of the testimony is not limited to physical healing. It happens with healed marriages, deliverance from torments and addictions, financial provision, and more. To always keep God's activities in our conversation is the wonderful privilege of God's people. Perhaps this is what was meant in God's instruction to Israel that they might *keep His testimony* as well as His commandments. (See Deut. 6:17.) Keeping the testimony is a part of the assignment we have been given and is the most practical way to sustain a revival long term.

Throughout church history, there have been great seasons of increase and seasons of decline. There have been seasons of the miraculous and then seasons with little to no supernatural activities among God's people. The absence of the supernatural is often blamed on God's sovereignty. I disagree. In Scripture, God lit the fire on the altar, but it was the priests that kept it burning. The responsibility to sustain a move of God falls on the shoulders of the priesthood of the believer, which is all who call Jesus Christ their Lord and Savior. It appears that one of the main ways we sustain a move of God and His supernatural activities among us is through our stewardship of His miraculous stories. It helps us to maintain an awareness of the God who invades the impossible, which dramatically changes how we do life.

One of my greatest privileges in life has been to minister alongside of Randy Clark. The miracles that happen during his meetings are stunning and life changing. They reveal God's heart in such a magnificent way that people leave knowing why they are alive, even when the miracles happened to someone else. What you will read on the following pages is but a small representation of what has become normal. This makes me happier than I can explain, that the activities of God among His people are being restored to biblical standards. My prayer is that these stories will become the fuel for the fires of revival to increase throughout all the earth! And that He would use you, the reader, in profound ways to spread the Good News with power to the whole world.

The Supernatural Power of a Testimony

In 1994 God put His hand on me, Randy Clark, an unknown pastor from a small church in St. Louis, to birth one of the greatest revival movements of the last half of the twentieth century. This move of God has resulted in the longest protracted revival meeting in the history of North America. Today, almost twenty-five years later, God's revival fire continues to burn and spread across the globe, expanding His Kingdom as thousands experience the Father's healing power and love. Salvations and rededications accompanied by miracles, signs and wonders, have resulted in tens of thousands of churches planted across forty different countries. I am humbled and awed daily by the scope and magnitude of God's great love and mercy. One of the most striking aspects of this mighty move of God is the incredible number of healings. As I look back over the past two decades I am continually amazed and delighted by God's desire to touch and heal people. At many of our meetings the healings happen so quickly and in such great number that it is impossible to record them all. As I began work on this journal of healing miracles I could not help but think of the apostle John's words, *"Jesus did many other things as well. If every one of them were written down, I suppose that even the whole world would not have room for the books that would be written"* (John 21:25).

What you will find within these pages are but a small sample of the thousands of miracles that have taken place in our gatherings. We tried to represent as best as possible the scope of God's love as it is reflected in healing, but of course our efforts are only a dim reflection of His greatness. There is such power in a miracle testimony. Jesus used testimony many times to confirm the truth of His words, knowing that testimony sustains and encourages us as we confront life in a fallen world. The early disciples had the Master, Jesus, with them. He is still with us today by His Spirit. Christ in us is the hope of glory, revealing His divine splendor and heavenly radiance as we participate with Him in the vigorous experience that is the empowered Christian life.

As you read through these testimonies you will see that they impact every physical part of the human body. Some of the testimonies sound rather simple and straightforward while others confront us with the reality that God indeed does perform creative miracles. Limbs grow out, cancerous tumors literally fall off, blind eyes see, those who were deaf and mute from birth suddenly hear and speak, withered limbs straighten and gain strength allowing the crippled to walk. Demons are cast out restoring physical, emotional and spiritual health where there was once decay and darkness, and broken bones miraculously heal. Every testimony brings fresh revelation of Jehovah-Rapha—the Lord who heals you (seeExod. 15:26b). This healing flows from the very nature of the Father because you cannot separate healing from God.

As if all of this were not exciting enough in and of itself, what is equally exciting is that we are allowed to participate in this revelatory ministry. Every believer is commissioned to heal the sick. Matthew 10:7-8 was Jesus's commission to His disciples when He walked upon the earth, and it is His commission to us today. His blood shed on the cross speaks a New Covenant word that gives us victory over sin and every disease. Testimonies of God's healing are in essence a victory shout.

Faith That Comes From Testimony

This is a book first and foremost about testimony, but to fully appreciate the power of the testimony we need an understanding of the faith that comes from testimony. Before we go any further, let's take a moment or two to unpack *faith*. Faith is the grace of God that causes His word to come alive in you, enabling your measure of confidence in Him to grow. When you see God loyal, staunch and steadfast in certain areas of your life, your measure of faith in those areas will increase. It's important to understand that there is a difference between the gift of faith and your measure of faith. While both are of the same nature, they are not created in the same way. Your measure of faith is your level of faith at any given time, whereas the gift of faith is given to you. The apostle Paul talks about the gift of faith in First Corinthians 12, telling us that it is a manifestation of God's grace, not an ability we possess. As Paul says, *"All these [gifts] are the work of one and the same Spirit, and he distributes them to each one, just as he determines"* (1 Cor. 12:11). A little farther along, in chapter 13, Paul shows us a more excellent way to move in the gifts, telling us that true faith expresses itself by love to God and others, not adherence to the law. Your trust and confidence in God—your faith—will grow when you study His Word, as the Holy Spirit illuminates His truths in your mind.

Sound teaching of Scripture brings an understanding of the ways of God and helps create faith instead of curiosity. People may see someone operate in the gift of healing, but without a solid Biblical understanding of what is happening, they likely won't be able to appreciate that what they are seeing is of God. They need to be taught the ways of God so that they can approach His supernatural manifestations with a sanctified intellect. Ultimately faith is not about our ability to believe God. It is God's ability to bring us into a place of belief in Him. A few years ago I was having a discussion with New Testament scholar, Dr. Craig Keener. We were talking about the difference between having faith *in* God and faith *of* God. Greek translations of Scripture tend to lean towards faith *in* God, probably because the majority of Greek scholars were not healing evangelists. The context of their experience governed their interpretation. You can't really understand how faith can come from God unless you have experienced it. For this reason, I make it a point to teach before I minister healing. In this way I till the soil in the hearts of those present so God's seeds of faith can fall on fertile ground. I would much rather take time to teach than see emotion or desperation or curiosity take the place of faith.

Early on in my ministry, God began using words of knowledge to increase the level of faith in me and in those I was ministering to. A word of knowledge is a rhema word from the Holy Spirit. Such words are always consistent with the will of God, and when declared, they can shift the atmosphere. Before and during ministry time I would get all sorts of physical aches and pains that were not natural to my physical body. At first I often hesitated to share these words of knowledge in my meetings because I didn't fully understand the concept, but as my knowledge and confidence in my ability to hear from God in this way increased, I would share and see people healed. Without fail, every time a word of knowledge brought healing, the faith in the room would increase. Now words of knowledge are an integral part of my ministry. Oftentimes, people are healed just by hearing a word of knowledge without anyone praying for them because the faith of God had taken hold in them. You will find a number of testimonies in this book that give witness to the power of words of knowledge.

The Power of Testimony As Prophetic Revelation

While healing reveals the heart of God, it was and is also prophetic revelation of Jesus Christ. The Old Testament prophet Isaiah declared that mankind would know the true Messiah by the preaching of the good news to the poor accompanied by demonstrations of power (miracles, signs and wonders) that validated His Messianic ministry, (see Isa. 35:3-6) and that is exactly what happened. Jesus came on the scene and everything changed. Jesus the Messiah continues to reveal Himself today in the same way—through the preaching of the good news of the Gospel, and through miracles, signs and wonders. In fact, every testimony of a healing miracle is a fresh revelation of God in Jesus Christ. Healing and deliverance are as essential to the Gospel as the actual proclamation of the message. Revelation 19:10 says that the testimony of Jesus is the spirit of prophecy. Prophecy is an invitation for repetition, because what God has done, He will do again. This is why I believe we need to build a culture that understands the power of testimony. Some have trouble with this concept because they misunderstand what it means. Sharing testimony doesn't demonstrate a lack of humility because it's not about what we have done; it's about what God has done. The Old Testament tells us to keep the law, keep the statutes, and keep the testimonies. We are to testify to His mighty works. Testimonies of healings and miracles increase faith and release prophetic revelation.

Testimony and the Glory of God

There is a direct correlation between testimony and the glory of God. In fact, the number-one way God glorifies His name is through the sharing of testimony. Put another way, the most significant way in which God reveals His glory is through what He does—through His mighty acts. The Bible is so replete with His supernatural deeds that it is impossible to read it and miss God's glory. One of the mightiest demonstrations of God's glory was the gift of His Son. *"The Word became flesh and made his dwelling among us. We have seen his glory, the glory of the one and only Son, who came from the Father, full of grace and truth"* (John 1:14). The writer of Hebrews put it thus, *"The Son is the radiance of God's glory and the exact representation of his being, sustaining all things by his powerful word"* (Heb. 1:3).

The life and ministry of Jesus was characterized by supernatural deeds, all of which were intended to bring glory to God. In chapter 5 of the gospel of Mark, Jesus has just driven out a legion of demons from a man who was living among the tombs. Upon being set free, the man begs to go with Jesus, but Jesus has another assignment for him. He doesn't intend for this particular man to become a disciple but rather an evangelist, telling him to go and share his testimony. Jesus has instructed the church to continue to minister with miracles, signs and wonders today followed by testimony, both as a way to show God's great love and to bring Him glory.

Second Corinthians 4:13 says, *"It is written, 'I believed; therefore I have spoken.' Since we have that same spirit of faith, we also believe and therefore speak."* Paul is quoting David here but what I hear him saying is that as believers we need to live with the kind of faith that motivates outspokenness without regard to the consequences. We should be living with the certainty (the faith) that the One who raised Jesus from the dead will also raise us with Jesus (2 Cor. 4:14), and that He will touch us today with miracles, signs and wonders. We should never be embarrassed by our testimonies. I think we are taking away from God's glory if we do not testify to His mighty deeds. We must be motivated to be a charismatic people out of a desire to glorify God.

Ministering Out of Intimacy and Obedience

I believe it is the responsibility of every believer to do as much as possible to learn about the ways of God because that is how we will be able to draw close to His heart. In His Upper Room Discourse, Jesus tells His disciples that they are no longer servants but friends (see John 15:15) because He knows that it is out of relationship we minister. He modeled this for us in His relationship with the Father. Jesus is inviting us into an intimate relationship between Father, Son and Holy Spirit, to embrace His mission and do what He did. In this place of intimacy we will find His revelation. John 14:26 says, *"But the Advocate, the Holy Spirit, whom the Father will send in my name, will teach you all things and will remind you of everything I have said to you.*" Through the Spirit, Jesus is with us, and His Spirit enables us to do the same things He did and more (see John 14:12). Servants don't receive this kind of revelation, but friends do. The basis of supernatural faith is this revelation that flows from intimacy.

I want to touch briefly on the connection between obedience, intimacy, and revelation as it relates to healing. In the New Testament we find Jesus giving His disciples the secrets of His power and His relationship with the Father that grew out of His (Jesus's) obedience. Because Jesus was perfectly obedient to the Father, there was nothing that hindered His ability to see and hear what the Father was doing. Revelation flowed to Him from the heart of the Father. Jesus says, "If you love me, you will obey what I command (see John 14:15). We are not saved by obedience, but we can have intimacy with Jesus if we obey Him. Understand, the kind of obedience Jesus is talking about is not possible apart from the renewing and regenerating work of the Holy Spirit in us.

Let's take faith, obedience, intimacy, revelation, healing and testimony a step further as found in Scripture. In John 15:4-8 Jesus talks about the vine and the braches, and how, apart from Him we can bear no fruit. Then He says that it is to the Father's glory that we bear much fruit. The fruit Jesus is speaking of here is the fruit of "doing." He is saying that we can bear much fruit from the works we do that can only be accomplished in the power of His Spirit. In other words, anything done in the flesh does not bring God glory, but what is done in the power of the Spirit brings God great glory. So it follows that we can and should bring God glory by ministering healing and deliverance in His name. Jesus certainly did this, and He did it out of intimacy and obedience. Jesus was constantly abiding with the Father, so much so that God's glorious power actually emanated around Him and flowed through Him. This is why the woman with the issues of bleeding was healed when she touched the hem of His garment (see Mark 5:29).

You'll notice from verse 30 that Jesus wanted the woman to come forward and testify to her healing. He knew that faith was at work in this woman, and it was her faith that had healed her (see Mark 5:34). The atmosphere of the crowd shifted when this woman testified to her healing, and when Jesus acknowledged her faith. This loving act of God's power and glory was a demonstration of the Kingdom of God that came to earth with Jesus (see Mark 5:34).

As you read through these testimonies, you'll encounter victory upon victory. You'll see that the ones praying for healing were as profoundly impacted by God's healing touch as those who are healed. With every victory, the Kingdom of God advances on the earth. When Jesus began His ministry in Galilee, He announced His identity when He said, *"The time is fulfilled, and the kingdom of God is at hand. Repent and believe in the gospel"* (Mark 1:15 NKJV). This declaration ushered in His Kairos time, and that Kairos time is still ongoing. As we continue to be obedient to the Great Commission, seeking intimacy with the Giver first and foremost, He comes in power, showing Himself glorious above all things on earth and in Heaven. He is truly the vine, and if we will become His branches, He will bear fruit in us and through us as we draw close to His heart, embracing the great command to love one another as Christ loves us, and allowing God to create the atmosphere for the miraculous to flow.

CANCER

Cancer is a term for a group of diseases that demonstrate abnormal cell growth. Cancerous diseases can metastasize to any part of the body. The World Health Organization lists cancer as the leading cause of death worldwide.[2]

Surely He took up our pain and bore our suffering, yet we considered Him punished by God, stricken by Him, and afflicted. But He was pierced for our transgressions, He was crushed for our iniquities; the punishment that brought us peace was on Him, and by His wounds we are healed.
—ISAIAH 53:4-5

---

2 "Cancer," *World Health Organization*, accessed June 1, 2017, http://www.who
.int/mediacentre/factsheets/fs297/en/.

Brain Tumor; Breast Cancer; Abdominal Cancer

We had a ministry in my church to go to the poor to pray and minister to the sick. I expect the greatest miracles among the lost and poor because they are so needy.

I was with a team one day, praying for people, when I was told about a woman there who was dying of cancer. Her name was Terry. She was a beautiful blonde-haired lady about twenty-five years old. She had two daughters that were five and seven from a previous marriage. She had been living with a man who had recently stolen her car, emptied her bank account, taken all her cash, and run off. She felt rejected by her divorce, and now she felt rejected by the man she had been living with out of wedlock. On top of all that, she was dying of an inoperable brain tumor. This tumor had metastasized into the tissue in her breast and spread down to the abdominal tract. The doctors said there was nothing more they could do, that the tumor was inoperable. They told her to go home and make her will out because she was going to die.

When I learned of all this, I asked Terry if I could pray for her, and she said, "Yes." When I started to put my hands on her head, she drew back and said, "What are you doing?"

"You said I could pray for you. That is what I'm doing," I replied.

"Here? Now?" she said.

"Yes," I replied.

"I don't think so" was her response. She thought I was going to go home and pray for her. She didn't understand that I intended to pray for her right then and there, but she finally let me pray. As I prayed, she began to feel heat on her head, and then electricity going through her head. I felt as though God said to me, "This one is on Me."

Every two weeks, we took food to Terry and prayed for her. We did this about six times over a twelve-week period. Then one day she called me and told me not to come back, that she didn't need us to bring food anymore. I found out later that another man had moved in.

Several years went by, and then I saw her one day at the local food bank. "Terry, you're alive!" I shouted across the room. As we talked, she told me what had happened to her since I had last seen her. About six or eight weeks after our last visit, she went to the doctor. Both an MRI and a full-body scan revealed no cancer. "I had always wondered if it had anything to do with you praying for me," she said.

"Terry, Jesus healed you," I replied.

I was able to get Terry to come to our church, where she gave her testimony of what God had done for her.

Told by Randy Clark in a sermon titled
"The Thrill of Victory"

Breast Cancer; Deliverance

I was at a church in Sao Paulo, Brazil, with a Global Awakening Youth Power Invasion team. At one point I saw a woman in the back manifesting strongly. I went back to her and ministered deliverance and then found out that she had a tumor in each breast. Both were cancerous. Many women in her family had the same thing. I knew the Lord was about to make a miracle happen. I began to pray, and after about twenty minutes I asked her if the tumors were gone. Through the translator she told me she would be right back, that she was going to the bathroom to check. We anxiously waited for her to come out, and when she did, she was jumping and screaming, crying, and just going crazy. She ran over to us, grabbed me, and squeezed me tight. Both the tumors were completely gone! There was no sign of them anywhere! For the rest of the night she cried and smiled.

Michael, age seventeen
Global Awakening Youth Power Invasion
trip to Sao Paulo, Brazil

Breast Cancer

I was on a Global Awakening trip to Brazil. One day I prayed for a young woman who had a tumor in her right breast. She told me it was the size of a walnut. I began praying for her, and as the power of God hit her, she fell to the floor. I continued to pray while she was on the ground. When she sat up, she checked the spot on her breast, and the tumor was gone! Her eyes got so big! She then stuck her hand down her shirt to double check and cried, "It is gone!" The look on her face was precious. I will never forget it. I told her to raise her hands to Heaven and thank God for her healing. "I love Jesus," she cried. "Jesus loves you," I replied.

This was my first mission trip. I came in desperation, seeking God and to be used by God. I was so concerned that God wouldn't use me, but He sure did! This healing happened on the second day of the trip. Praise God!

Sharon
Global Awakening mission trip to Brazil

Breast Cancer; Back Pain

Today during the morning meeting I had the opportunity to pray for a girl who had a lump in her breast that reached around to her back. When I first started praying, I felt nothing, she felt nothing, and there were no manifestations. As we continued to pray, she said she felt her shoulder and arm go numb. I blessed what God was doing in Jesus's name, and then she checked and the lump was gone! The look on her face and in her eyes was utter astonishment. She was overwhelmed that she was healed. It was awesome to see her realize that God had healed her. Then I prayed for an impartation of the Holy Spirit, and God blasted her! How fun! Glory to God! I also prayed for a hurt knee and God completely healed it. The coolest part is that I was not feeling super holy or anointed. It was just me asking God to heal, and He did. Praise God! He is faithful.

Julie
Global Awakening mission trip to Manaus, Brazil

Breast Cancer; Back Pain; Salvation

Right after we all received impartation from Randy Clark, Gary Oates, and the rest, I went to the healing tent and I saw so many miracles! An elderly lady came for prayer. She had a cancerous tumor in her breast and pain in her back. We asked if she was a Christian, and she said she was not and she didn't want to be one unless God could heal her. We thought it was the perfect opportunity for God to be glorified so we started praying. We called down the fire of Heaven to consume her and heal her. We commanded the tumor to disappear and the pain in her back to leave. The Holy Spirit came heavily upon her and she fell down under the power of the Spirit. She got up a few minutes later and we asked her to check and see if the tumor was gone and to move around and see if her back pain was completely gone. She checked and her back pain was totally gone and the lump in her breast had completely disappeared! We praised God and asked if she wanted to receive Christ as her Savior. She said "Yes!" with great joy and excitement. We led her in the salvation prayer and asked God to bless her.

April and Catrina
Global Awakening mission trip to Belém, Brazil

Breast Cancer; Uterine Problems

We were with Randy Clark at the local church in Belém, Brazil, on the last night of our mission trip. God's presence was strong in the meeting. Many people were healed. A woman came seeking prayer for a tumor and problems in her uterus. She had a tumor the size of an egg underneath her left breast. As we prayed, I felt the tumor grow smaller and softer. She didn't seem to think there was much change (just a little) so we prayed over her abdomen. She suddenly began to vibrate, and a spontaneous prayer language came out of her mouth. I asked the interpreter what was happening and she told us that the woman was feeling electricity shooting into her body. We checked for the tumor and it was gone! She was excited and started speaking very fast to the interpreter, who told us that the woman actually felt her uterus and ovaries "pulled up" into place in her body!!! Praise God.

Julie
Global Awakening mission trip to Belém, Brazil

Cancer

This is my favorite testimony from our mission trip to Ukraine. We had been praying for the dancers, and my translator was just giving them a final blessing when I noticed a woman wanting prayer. I called my translator for help. Just then an usher came over with a young teenage boy; he had just been saved that night and they wanted me to pray for him. I asked the boy to wait just a few minutes, as I needed to pray for this other woman first. He stood by while the woman told us that she wanted prayer for advanced cancer. As I got ready to pray, God told me to have the boy pray for her. I knew he had the Holy Spirit because he had been saved earlier in the evening. Through the translator I asked the boy if he heard what the woman needed, and he said, "Yes." I told him that he could help her. The woman interrupted and told the translator that the boy was only saved that night, indicating that she wanted us to pray for her, not the boy. I understood that because she had advanced cancer, she wanted the best prayer that she could get, so I tried to reassure her that the boy carried the same authority to pray for her healing as we did. Then I had the boy place his hand on her and just ask God to help her. He seemed to go right at it, saying a simple prayer, and God began to touch her immediately! When the boy finished praying,

I continued to pray and bless what God was doing, and then I asked my anointed translator to pray for the boy. God continued to touch the woman with powerful waves that shook her for quite some time. I prayed in Russian, "More, Lord—go deeper, Lord—more anointing for healing—be healed in the name of Jesus." When the shaking subsided, I brought the translator back and asked how the woman was doing. She said that all her pain was now gone. God had done something very powerful. She was going to check with her doctors, but she felt that she was healed. She was very happy, thanking me as we praised God together. Then I reminded her that it was the boy who had prayed for her first. She turned to him with tears and grabbed his hand, thanking him and blessing his life. Now that's the way to start a life with Jesus. Thank You, Father; You are so good!

Don
Global Awakening mission trip to Ukraine

Cancer—Tumor on Upper Chest; Knee Pain

Four of us on the team prayed for a preacher's mother-in-law who had terminal cancer, with a tumor on her upper chest. I asked her daughter if she was a Christian, and they said they did not think so. I asked her if she knew Jesus and believed in Him, and she said she did. I prayed for the Holy Spirit to show her any area for which she needed to ask God for forgiveness, or if there was anyone she needed to forgive. After a minute or so, she said, "No." We then started praying for the tumor and cancer to leave. (There was pain in the tumor.) After praying for a few minutes, we asked how she was doing, and she said the pain was gone and the tumor had shrunk a little bit. We prayed more, and the tumor shrank a little more. (It had been the size of a golf ball cut in half and now was the size of a nickel.) We continued to pray until the tumor was almost gone. We then prayed for her knee that hurt from the cancer. The pain made it difficult for her to walk. She said she felt heat in her knee, and then the pain left. We told her to get up and walk around. She did, and it was 50 percent better. We prayed again and then asked her to check it out. She did, and her eyes got big! She said it was 100 percent better and she was walking fine, without any limp. We then prayed a little more for the tumor, and it disappeared completely! I told her daughter to pray for her every day with the laying on of hands. They were all so happy, hugging and crying. Thank You, Jesus!

Bob
Environmental Staff Technician
Global Awakening mission trip to Brazil

Fallopian Tube Tumor

We were at a church one night, and Randy was ministering. He had received a word from the Lord that there was a pool of healing in the front of the church. A lot of people went up for prayer for healing— so many that we had to direct people to the back for prayer. A woman approached me with her daughter. She explained that she had a tumor in one of her female organs (her fallopian tube) and that she had six months to live. She had undergone five surgeries in five years for cancer. The interpreter and I prayed for her, asking the Lord to come with His healing fire. We continued to pray and intercede, and after a few minutes we asked her if there was any change. She said she felt fire in the area of the tumor and that the pain had decreased. We continued to pray for her. A few moments later, we asked again if there was a change, and she said the pain was gone. When she checked for the tumor, she could not feel it. She double-checked and moved around a bit to test her body. She believes she was healed, and so do I! Praise God!!

Elise, age eighteen
Global Awakening Youth Power Invasion
trip to Curitiba, Brazil

Lung Cancer—Pancoast Tumor

Three of us on the team prayed for a diabetic man who had undergone an amputation. He had a tumor in his lung that made it difficult to move his right arm. He also had chest pain and swelling in his right hand. As we were praying, a Brazilian physician came up to observe. He spoke to the wife and got more information and told me that the tumor was a "Pancoast tumor." I was focused on the foot at the time so I didn't discuss it with him much further. I vaguely remembered learning about Pancoast tumors in medical school but couldn't remember if they were benign or malignant, or what made them unusual. When I got home, I looked up Pancoast tumors. They are highly malignant lung cancers that usually grow in the top part of the lung (the apex). They aggressively extend locally, and two of their hallmarks are that they tend to grow through the lung into the chest wall (causing chest pain) and down into a major nerve plexus of the arm called the brachial plexus. The brachial plexus receives the nerves coming off of the lower cervical spinal cord. These nerves control the movement and sensation of the arm. When this plexus has been damaged, the person may be unable to move the arm and may have decreased sensation and severe pain, depending on the extent of the damage. The tumor can also grow into the lymphatic system and cause obstruction, which then causes swelling below the level of the obstruction. Pancoast tumors have a very high mortality rate. Most people die within eight months if the cancer is left untreated. Even with "successful" treatment, which involves removal of most of the lung surrounding the tumor, followed by chemo and/or radiation, survival at five years is only about 35–40 percent. Most of these tumors cannot be removed surgically if they are first identified after a person begins to experience symptoms because they have already spread beyond surgical resection by the time symptoms begin to appear.

When I read this, I had a renewed sense of awe at what the Lord did for that man, particularly as our focus was less on the tumor than it was on the diabetes and the leg and foot pain. Assuming that this man's symptoms in his arm and chest were a direct result of the tumor's invasion into those areas, the radical improvement in his symptoms (arm movement, loss of pain in the arm and chest, decreased swelling in his hand) is then a direct result of the Lord rapidly shrinking the tumor, removing it from the brachial plexus, lymphatic system, and chest wall. Amen! It is very likely that, prior to our praying, the man had less than eight months to live, given that he was already significantly symptomatic and probably not a candidate for surgery (even if that option was available to him under the Brazilian medical system—which it probably wasn't because his diabetes was not being treated). Even without having followed up on his diabetes and gangrene, I believe we can say with confidence that the Lord was healing his cancer.

Laurie
Global Awakening mission trip to Brazil

Pancreatic Cancer

I was in the largest Assemblies of God church in Kentucky when a man named Tony came up to me. He was twenty-three years old and worked as a nurse. Even though he was in an Assemblies of God church, he hadn't been to many Pentecostal-type services. Tony had been diagnosed with pancreatic cancer about six months prior and had undergone all the available medical treatments, to no avail. He was yellow, skinny, and looked like a skeleton wrapped in skin. He weighed about eighty pounds, had no hair, had dark circles under his eyes, and had less than a month to live.

Before I prayed for him, I explained to him what he might feel during the prayer time. I told him he might feel fire and electricity in his body or he might feel nothing. I asked him to let us know if he felt anything. As I began to pray, his eyelids began to flutter very fast. Waves of healing began to go through him. After the first wave, he started to get up, thinking the prayer time was over. I explained that God often comes in waves when He is healing and advised him to just lie there for a little longer so that God could continue to heal him. Sure enough, more healing waves of Jesus began to flow over his body. We prayed for him for three days, three times a day, as waves of healing continued to wash over his body. While in worship one night, a fireball from Heaven came and hit him in his head, and he felt the healing power of Jesus come into his head. When he went back to the doctor, they found he was totally healed of cancer. As a result of this experience he went on to become an evangelist.

Told by Randy Clark in a sermon titled
"The Thrill of Victory"

Stomach Cancer

There was an older woman, maybe sixty years of age, who had stomach cancer and a severely swollen abdomen. She was in intense pain and had been written off by the doctors. The team had prayed for her several days earlier, and she was now able to sit up and move about, whereas she had previously been bedridden with pain. Several members of the ministry team prayed for her again before the service, but she was still experiencing pain and swelling. When the preaching ended and words of knowledge began, she was standing next to her husband. I started to pray for him, and Doug started to pray for her. God touched them both. She fell under the power of God (face down) and cried out. Doug and I continued to pray over her, and she cried out several times. Her body grew very hot, and she started to tremble. As we continued to pray, God's peace came over her. She eventually pushed herself up and proclaimed that the pain was totally gone and the swelling was gone. She grabbed my hand and put it on her stomach. Her stomach was normal, without swelling or hardness. She started to walk and jump and praise God. She stood up before the congregation, who all knew her condition, and testified. Everyone praised God!

Roy
Retired Airline Pilot
Global Awakening mission trip to Cuba

Stomach Cancer; Bone Cancer; Salvation

Here is the testimony of the healing of a young man, the grandson of a high Brazilian government official. A team of four of us (Brent, Suzanne, Eddie, and Juliana) went to a hospital in Goiânia to pray for him. He was a thirty-five-year-old man with cancer that had eaten away at his stomach (part of it was already removed) and spread to his spine. He was so sick that he was unable to swallow his own saliva. He was a shell of a man with pasty, pale skin. He lay there sunken into his bed and weakly greeted us. His wife was there—a woman of great faith who believed God for his healing. We shared some of the wonderful testimonies of God's miraculous power, and then we talked with him about how the Lord wanted to heal him because of His great love. Then we prayed for healing. As we prayed, he felt the fire of God in his stomach and also felt great peace. We then asked him if he had ever received Jesus as his Lord. He had not but was willing so I led him in a prayer for salvation and to be filled with the Holy Spirit. His wife, who had been crying out for him for years, was weeping with joy. By the time we left, which was about thirty to forty-five minutes later, his countenance had completely changed. His color was much better, and he got up and gave us all hugs before we left. The next day, I received a call that he was home, not because the hospital sent him home to die, but because he had told his wife, "Jesus has healed me! Let's go home!" I was able to talk with him and found out that several hours after we left, he was eating food! He said that he was feeling so much better and expected that he would be feeling better every day. He said that when we prayed, his wife felt the angels in his hospital room. He also told us that he would come to America to share his testimony of God's miraculous healing. Jesus, to You we give all the glory!!!

Brent and Suzanne
Global Awakening mission trip to Goiânia, Brazil

Uterine Tumors; Breast Tumors; Forgiveness

An elderly woman had a tumor the size of a large egg on her uterus. Through the interpreter we prayed for God's power to come and heal her. We asked for the holy fire of God to burn the tumor off and commanded the tumor to go. After a couple of minutes of similar prayers, we asked if she felt any change. She looked surprised as she felt around for the tumor. The woman told us that it had shrunk considerably. I got excited and felt increase for God to complete the healing. We prayed again, breaking off any curses spoken over her. We asked for more power, more fire, more healing. We kept repeating these simple prayers. After a couple of minutes, she checked and it was down to the size of a quarter. I felt led to ask her to forgive her father. I didn't need to know why because God knew. Shortly after the woman prayed and forgave her father, the tumor disappeared completely!

That same day, a pregnant woman with a tumor in her right breast came to me for prayer. I invited the elderly lady who had been healed of the tumor in her uterus to pray with us. We shared her testimony so as to increase the faith of the pregnant woman. We began by prophesying over the unborn child. There were many details that the Lord wanted to address about this boy she was carrying. She confirmed everything while streams of tears flowed down her face. Four doctors had advised her to abort the baby because of the tumor, but she said, "No, I am going to have this baby and dedicate it to the Lord." We prayed very simply for the Holy Spirit to come and heal. We commanded the tumor to go and for the fire to come, and then we asked her to check the tumor. A look of surprise came over her face, and she began to get excited. She said it had shrunk from the size of a half dollar coin to the size of a nickel. We prayed again, and it shrank to the size of a dime. I felt that the final healing would take place when she had forgiven her husband. She confirmed that she had not forgiven him. After she had a mighty encounter with Jesus in the forgiveness process, I interrupted her weeping to suggest that she check the tumor again. She checked and kept searching around for it. It had disappeared 100 percent when she forgave her husband.

Wendy
Office Manager
Global Awakening mission trip to Rio de Janeiro, Brazil

CIRCULATORY SYSTEM

THE CIRCULATORY SYSTEM is an organ system consisting of the heart, arteries, and veins that circulates blood throughout the body, transporting nutrients, oxygen, carbon dioxide, hormones, and blood cells. It includes fetal circulation via the placenta. It is comprised of the cardiovascular system and the lymphatic system. The actions of the circulatory system provide nourishment and aid in fighting diseases.

Create in me a pure heart, O God, and
renew a steadfast spirit within me.
—PSALM 51:10

Chest Pain

During our trip, Yolanda, the lady that made all of our arrangements for our team's transportation and meals, was experiencing severe chest pain. Her pain was a "10" on a scale of 1–10. Because I am a nurse, someone came and got me out of a meeting to check on her. I found her clutching her chest. She was clammy. Her pulse was regular. She said that she was short of breath. I commanded the spasm of the coronary artery to release and declared the blood flow to be normal, all in the name of Jesus. I spoke ease to the respirations. After the prayer, I asked her how she was. The pain was now a "3" out of 10. We continued to pray for another minute or two, commanding the fear and panic to leave until all the pain and shortness of breath were completely gone. Before we prayed, she had felt like she was going to die. Now she felt good and was smiling.

Lynette
Registered Nurse
Global Awakening mission trip to Mexico

Circulation Issues—Legs; Pain in Knee, Ankle, and Hip

On a Youth Power Invasion trip to Brazil, I prayed for a woman named Shirley. She told me she had circulation problems in her legs, making it difficult for her to stand for long periods of time due to the pain. My translator and I prayed for her; then we asked if she felt any better. She indicated that the pain was a little better. We prayed more and asked again, and she said that her knee hurt more! We continued to pray, and eventually the pain in her knee was gone. Her knee was better, and so was her ankle; but her hip still hurt. I asked her if she wanted to stand up, and she did. I prayed for her again, and then she started jumping and jumping and jumping! It was so exciting! I asked her what happened, and she said the pain was gone! "Glory to God" was shared by all present. It was so cool.

Lacey, age seventeen
Global Awakening Youth Power Invasion
trip to Curitiba, Brazil

Congestive Heart Failure

I so greatly appreciate those who have been standing with me in faith for my healing. So many have told me they are praying and have contacted me with Scriptures and things God has said to them regarding my recovery, so I thought I'd give an update about the most recent developments.

As some of you may recall, about two years ago my nephrologist wanted me to do a workup for a possible kidney transplant. I hadn't decided whether the transplant was what I was going to do or not, but I submitted to the workup anyway. After the cardiologist looked at the tests, he told me that I should consider a double transplant—heart and kidney!

Of course, I was shocked and troubled. One thing I knew was that I didn't want a heart transplant. The cardiologist's "sales pitch" for the heart transplant was quite bleak—something like, "If you have it, you might live ten years; and if you don't, you still might live ten years." Not very convincing!

He put me on heart medication and said to come back in six months. During this time, a friend called me and said he'd been praying for me and felt that God had told him that He (God) was going to heal me from the inside out and that my heart would be healed first. When the six months were up, I went to see the cardiologist again and was delighted to hear him say that if he didn't know I'd had heart problems, he wouldn't suspect it today. His examination was only superficial so we agreed that I would come back in six months for a full round of tests on the heart.

The normal ejection fraction of the heart muscle (the percentage of the blood pumped each beat) is 55 percent. When I was first examined, my ejection fraction was 15 percent. A fellow minister shared with me that he had the same problem, and when the doctor saw that his ejection fraction was 15 percent, he said, "It's a wonder that you are even up and around." Although I am sometimes tired in the afternoons, I have continued to work throughout this whole battle.

When the time came, I went back for the full round of tests. The results were encouraging. My ejection fraction was now 45 percent, which is on the low side of normal. I was certainly glad I hadn't seriously considered a heart transplant! Now this news alone would be cause for rejoicing and is in itself a good testimony. But there's more. About a month and a half ago, I was having trouble sleeping and was plagued with severe headaches. I had been diagnosed with sleep apnea and was suffering from the effects of it. My lack of sleep was making me nauseous, and anti-nausea medications were affecting me negatively. After two days of no sleep and an inability to keep food down, my doctor told me to check into the hospital. I was having symptoms that resembled a heart attack or a stroke, and she didn't want me to take any chances.

I checked in and prepared for a fresh round of tests, wondering if perhaps my heart had turned around and I was facing congestive heart failure again. They ran a large battery of tests, and then I waited for the results. God met me during my time at the hospital, and I wasn't particularly fearful, just curious. When the results came back, my ejection fraction was now 55 percent—perfectly normal! None of the other tests brought bad news either. I am trusting God to heal my pancreas and my kidneys. Thanks be to God, who always leads us in triumph in Christ!

I recently spoke at a Randy Clark Healing School in Milford, Ohio. Pam and I really enjoy getting to be a part of these schools. We are in such agreement with Randy's vision of equipping the saints and releasing them to minister. As I finished my first two sessions, a woman came up to me who was obviously quite moved by what God was showing her. She struck me as an intelligent, mature woman, not the least bit flighty. I asked her to write down what God had shown her. Here is what she wrote:

> Being a cardiac nurse [her husband is a cardiologist] I knew that when you said your ejection fraction went from 15 percent to 60 percent and that your thallium stress test did not show any ischemia [a deficiency in the supply of blood due to an obstruction] that you obviously had a sovereign work of God. When I initially saw you on the platform, I felt you had some medical problems. As you continued to minister, I began to see visions with my eyes open, which I have never had. I have only had visions with my eyes closed. But I began to see a kidney—reddish purple and plump and healthy. For about five minutes, this picture persisted. Then I saw a sword being forced into your belly. I immediately knew it was the sword of the Lord to bring healing to your inner organs. I forgot to tell you [when she first related this to me] that the Lord said He was going to cut out the bad parts and give you new parts. Then I saw your pancreas explode in many pieces and then I saw a new pancreas.

As you might imagine, her words were very encouraging to me!! When my doctor gave me the cardiac report, he didn't indicate how unusual this was. He acted like it was good but not unusual. So I didn't realize what a miracle God has done for my heart. I think He wanted me to know so He sent this well-qualified lady to inform me! God is good!

Joe McIntyre

Heart Problems

Tom Jones taught on words of knowledge and then allowed a couple of minutes to pass before asking for anyone who had not previously given a word of knowledge to come up and give whatever they had received. The first man to come up said he saw a man with a blue shirt with a red stripe who had a heart problem. No one responded. Then, one of the interpreters pointed out that Tom's interpreter was wearing a navy blue shirt with a stripe!! When asked, the interpreter said he did have a heart problem. He was prayed for and then came up to the front to testify to his healing, which was accompanied by manifestations. He felt relief in his chest. It was amazing to see God use the first accurate word of knowledge right at the start of the session.

Peter
Corporate Finance
Global Awakening mission trip to Brazil

Heart Problems

During lunch one day, the team was given the option of signing up in groups of three (two team members and one translator) to minister to those church leaders who desired further ministry. My wife Rachel and I signed up. During this ministry time, we ministered with a sweet translator named Jennifer. The Spirit of God was flowing in such synergy and power. We prayed for a woman who had been experiencing heart problems for years. We laid hands on her and commanded her heart to be healed in Jesus's name. Her face suddenly changed from a serious, focused waiting (with her eyes closed and a blank expression on her face) to a wide-eyed look of total joy. Then she exclaimed, "I know I am healed!" On our last day with this particular group, the woman reported 100 percent healing of her heart condition and that she had not experienced any of the symptoms that had regularly plagued her. Praise the King of Glory!

James
Personal Trainer
Global Awakening mission trip to China

High Blood Pressure

My name is Laurie, and I attended one of your healing schools in Nashville. I just wanted to give a praise report. I was healed of high blood pressure at the meeting on Thursday night. The Lord is so good! A little over a year ago, I had a terrible headache that lasted several days. I went to the doctor, and he said my blood pressure was high—157/101. He put me on medication, but it made me feel horrible, like I was in a fog, so I stopped taking it. I did some research, stopped consuming a lot of caffeine, and tried to be consistent with exercise and diet. My blood pressure came down some but was still high. On Thursday night at the healing school, you talked about the woman with the issue of blood and how she felt that if she could only touch the hem of the Lord's garment, she would be healed. You asked for those with blood issues to stand. I did, and I felt the Lord's presence in such a sweet way—no heat or bolts of lightning, but a real peace. I waved my hands to indicate that I felt I was healed. On Thursday of the following week, I had another doctor's appointment. My blood pressure was completely normal! He kept saying, "I can't figure this out." I told him about being prayed for, but he continued to say, "I can't figure this out." Thank you for ministering healing in the name of the Lord. I'm a worship leader. On Sunday we sang healing songs over the people. I gave my testimony, and people came for prayer. How neat is that! I will pray for your ministry and hope one day to take my family on one of your ministry trips.

Laurie
Global Awakening School of Healing
Nashville, Tennessee

Stroke

During one of the services, we prayed for a woman who was around seventy years of age. She had suffered a stroke, and she could not lift her right arm or walk unassisted. We prayed, and she was able to lift her arm halfway. We continued to pray, and she started to open and close her hand and was able to lift her arm higher. She also walked by herself without the use of a cane.

Pastor Kenton
Global Awakening mission trip to Brazil

Stroke

On a Global Awakening mission trip to Brazil, John and I prayed for an elderly lady who had suffered a stroke. She came in dragging her right leg. We prayed for quite a while, and little by little, she could use her leg and move it freely. Before our prayers, it would take her a long time to get up from her chair. After we prayed for her, she walked out of the church on her own. Yay, God!

Michelle
Scientist
Global Awakening mission trip to Brazil

DELIVERANCE

DELIVERANCE is a New Testament reality and is central to the ministry of healing that Jesus entrusted to His Church. He has given us the authority to minister deliverance by the finished work of the cross. *"And God raised us up with Christ and seated us with Him in the heavenly realms in Christ Jesus, in order that in the coming ages He might show the incomparable riches of His grace..."* (Eph. 2:6-7). As we stand in the place of victory with Christ, He gives us victory over the demonic, enabling us to be a continuing revelation of God's love and an integral part of the presentation of the Gospel.

When evening came, many who were demon-possessed were brought to Him, and He drove out the spirits with a word and healed all the sick.
—MATTHEW 8:16

Addiction

One of the delights of returning to a place in which you've ministered before is hearing and seeing the results of prayer. One result that blessed me came from a young woman who approached me with a huge grin, asking me if I remembered her. "I'm Vera," she said. "You prayed for me last year." I honestly didn't recognize her until she told me she'd asked for prayer for drug and alcohol addiction. I then realized that the healthy-looking woman glowing with God's love was the redeemed and restored, rather than the broken, desperate woman I'd prayed for last year. Wow! What a change. Yay, God! I remembered I'd prayed for her with a greater than usual confidence, knowing that God was intervening in her addiction that day.

Robbie
Global Awakening mission trip to Ukraine

Alcoholism; Salvation

After an incredibly anointed meeting in the morning, we went to lunch. At one point during the meal we asked our waiter if he had anything he wanted us to pray for, and he said yes, there was. He asked us to pray that he could get rid of his alcoholism, and he also wanted healing for his family. We rebuked the spirit of alcoholism and asked God to bring restoration to his family. After a while, we asked if he would like to know Jesus, the One who can help him. He said that he would like to know Jesus. He prayed right there and accepted Jesus. It was so awesome. Thank You, Jesus! Then we gave him directions to the church, and he said he would try to come. It was so amazing. God is so cool!

Rebecca and Rachel
Students
Global Awakening Youth Power Invasion
trip to Curitiba, Brazil

Alcoholism; Forgiveness; Emotional Healing

I prayed with a twelve-year-old girl whose parents just recently had separated. The mother blamed the girl for the problems in their marriage. I asked her if she had bitterness toward her parents and hurt from what her mother said to her father. She did, so we prayed and she forgave them and herself. We broke off the generational curse of alcoholism from her father and family. She also was healed emotionally when I informed her that she was a princess and that is the way her Heavenly Father sees her. I encouraged her to find a spiritual mother to help her during this time in her life. I met her pastor and wife, and they agreed that they would help find her such a woman.

Pastor Kenton
Global Awakening mission trip to Brazil

Anxiety and Confusion; Forgiveness

I would consider my life to be like that of many people: I grew up with a loving, devoted mother; siblings (with whom I don't always get along); and a brave stepfather (now deceased) who willingly embraced my mother and her three children. I lived in a home free of physical, sexual, and verbal abuse—no alcohol, drugs, gambling, or marital unfaithfulness. Together we attended church regularly and went on family vacations.

I am married to a hardworking husband of over twenty-five years. We have two beautiful, healthy, grown children; a comfortable home; and an active church life. For all intents and purposes I had a good life. I didn't know why I felt like such a mess, even to the point of feeling crazy at times. I didn't know what was wrong with me, and it seemed to get worse with each passing year. I had done all the things I knew how. I had accepted Christ at the age of twenty-two, was baptized in the Spirit soon after, and even attended counseling. I went on to attend numerous healing and prayer conferences. I even went through deliverance in the 1970s. All these efforts provided a period of peace and relief; however, it never lasted. I knew the necessity of forgiveness, praying, and serving the Lord with all of my heart, but I was hurting, lost, frustrated, scared, and downright angry. There was no spiritual fruit in my life. I kept asking, "Where are You, God? Do I have a purpose? How can You use me in this state, or will You even use me?" There were answers to these questions all along the way, but I was so bound up that I couldn't see or hear them.

Freedom came for me one day at my church in a trailer located on the church grounds that was used for counseling. I entered my session chained and bound—a spiritual wimp. Miraculously, I emerged a free person! However, the day this captive was set free was preceded by two weeks of prayer and introspection as I searched my heart and asked the Lord for clarity and honesty. I was asked to make a list of people that I needed to forgive and why I needed to forgive them. The process proved to be more difficult than expected. Every time I tried to write my list, I became confused and couldn't put anything down on paper. Consequently, I sought advice from my pastor. He understood and prayed for me that I would receive clarity, and he bound whatever was trying to hinder me from my task. Amazingly, that evening my thoughts were clear, and words flowed nonstop from my heart onto my paper.

During my deliverance session, I was surprised by my reactions to some of the things I had written and was now verbalizing. This became an indicator of unsuspected and unresolved trouble spots. Ultimately, my inner "house" was swept clean and filled with the holy presence of my Lord and Savior. Afterward, I felt happy and at peace. I also felt exhausted—I had been through six hours of spiritual surgery (deliverance and inner healing). I felt a sense of order, purity, and wholeness that I had never experienced before. Later, I couldn't help but wonder if this newfound peace and freedom would pass in time as it had always done before. Would I struggle with the same old garbage? Today, I am happy to say that I am free and at peace. I realize the importance of the ministry of deliverance. Christians need not live broken, empty, defeated, ho-hum lives. The Lord has a definite plan and purpose for His people. As for me, I know where I've been, I know how far I've come, and I know where my destiny lies.

Betty's testimony from Tom Hauser's *Breaking Free*

Back Pain; Word Curse; Forgiveness

An elderly gentleman asked for prayer for pain in his lower back. We prayed for a few minutes, and the pain left. He returned an hour later and said that the pain had come back again. This time, we began searching for answers to the onset of the pain. "How long have you had the pains?" we asked. "Eight years" was his response. When we asked him what happened eight years ago, he could think of nothing. Then God gave me a word of knowledge—"word curse"—which opened a long-locked door. The gentleman said that a Catholic neighbor had pronounced a curse on him that he would have much pain because of a religious offense. We prayed that the curse would be broken. He forgave the Catholic neighbor and blessed him. Then we prayed again for his healing, and almost immediately he was healed! Glory to God forever!

Rob and Judy
Global Awakening mission trip to Argentina

Brain Disorder; Sexual Sin; Witchcraft

A young woman with a child about six years old approached us during the ministry time. She wanted prayer for her child, Abbey Rose, who had some type of brain disorder. As we talked with the mother, we found out that Abbey Rose's father was heavily involved in witchcraft. The mother also shared she had never been married to Abbey's father and was no longer involved with him, as she was a Christian. We led Abbey's mother in a prayer renouncing witchcraft and sexual immorality and other areas she mentioned. On the following night, she came back to the meeting and testified that Abbey Rose had gone to school and for the first time ever was able to write her name. She was so excited that Abbey Rose's ability to communicate had greatly improved. Thank You, Jesus, for Your healing power!

John and Cathy
Global Awakening mission trip to Auckland, New Zealand

Breast Lump; Occult; Generational Curses of Infirmity

In 2005, I was on a mission trip in São Paulo, Brazil, with a Youth Power Invasion team from Global Awakening. I prayed for a woman who had a lump in her breast. She said that cancer ran in the family and she was afraid the lump was cancerous. I began praying with a translator, asking the Holy Spirit to come, then commanding the lump to leave in Jesus's name and the pain to go away. After praying for a while, I asked her to check to see if her pain was gone and if the lump was gone. She said the pain was gone but the lump was still there. We began breaking off generational curses of infirmity, and I asked her if she or a family member was involved with the occult. She said her dad had been for a little while. I broke those ties off in Jesus's name and began asking the Holy Spirit to come and fill her, at which point she started crying and feeling heat. Again I commanded the lump to leave in Jesus's name. After a little while of praying these commands I asked her if she felt the lump. She checked and said it was gone! I was so excited! We all got really happy, and she began laughing. My friend and I began praying for more joy and then watched as she was touched and filled with joy and laughter. We blessed her and were so amazed. This was the first tumor that had disappeared while I was praying. I was blown away.

Jennifer
Global Awakening Youth Power Invasion
trip to São Paulo, Brazil

Bullet Wounds; Spirits of Death, Perversion, Abandonment, and Rejection; Loss of Sensation in Feet and Hand; Hearing Loss; Vision Loss

I was in São Paulo, Brazil, with a Global Awakening team. In one of the meetings, as the team gave words of knowledge, a woman stood repeatedly for three different words. Randy asked for those who had physical problems for more than five years and had just been healed to stand. Again, this woman stood. Randy asked these people to come forward to share what they had been healed of. As this woman shared, it became apparent that she had many other areas in need of physical healing. Another team member and I were asked to minister over her for the rest of her healing.

As we began the interview process, we discovered that she was a believer and that she had been shot twelve times. Her son and her parents had hired an assassin to kill her so that they could get her money. It is a miracle she was alive. The bullets had gone through one of her ears, a jaw, one of her eyes, an arm, her thigh (four bullets there), and her chest and back. She still had a bullet in her chest near her heart and bullet fragments in one of her forearms. Eight months after the shooting, an angel had come and removed the bullet that had been in her back. She had a metal jaw on one side of her face and could barely open her mouth. The ear that had been shot was deaf, and the eye hit by the bullet was almost blind—she could only see light and shadow. God healed three places in her body as a result of the words of knowledge given without anyone praying for her. She still had pain all over her body. She also had no sensation in her feet, except for pain, and had little sensation in one of her hands.

She had a sordid personal and family history that included ongoing sins of murder, rage, abuse, theft, perversion, abandonment, rejection, occult practice, and occult worship. Both she and her family had been involved in at least twelve arenas of the occult, along with false religion worship. As we walked her through forgiveness, confession, repentance, and renunciation of all of these areas, she began to feel release. We then began to pray for full restoration and healing to come. She felt heat begin at her head and move down her body. Within a short time, all the pain in her body was gone. She also was beginning to feel sensation in her feet and in the one hand that had been impacted. She was able to open her mouth much wider than before. Her hearing was restored in her deaf ear, and she had 50 percent of the vision return in the eye that had been impacted by the shooting. We tested her several times to be sure. We had to leave, but we encouraged her to return the next night for more prayer. Glory to God for the incredible Healer He is!

Aurora P.
Global Awakening mission trip to São Paulo, Brazil

Bullet Wounds; Paralysis; Spirit of Death; Drugs

A pastor asked me to pray for William, a paralytic who had been shot fourteen times in a drug-related attempted murder. William was sitting in a plastic chair when I approached him. As I got close to him, I sensed that he was oppressed by demons. He began to manifest a demonic shaking. I said, "In the name of Jesus, you foul spirits, I command you to leave!" Immediately, he stopped shaking. I asked him if he believed that Jesus could heal him, and he said, "Yes." We started to pray for his healing, and after several minutes, I asked if he was ready to walk by himself up to the platform and give a testimony of God healing him. I told him not to use a cane or crutches or to allow anyone to help him. He was giddy as he wobbled up the aisle, gaining strength as he went. He climbed the steps to the platform unaided by anyone and gave testimony of his miracle, then collapsed to the floor. Glory to Jesus!

Rob
Home Builder
Global Awakening mission trip to Colombia

Childhood Abuse; Forgiveness

A team member asked me to go over to a lady in the crowd who remained after pastors and leaders had received prayer. "Check out her eyes, and tell me what you think," she said. The woman's eyes looked like she'd not slept in a long time, but they also had an eerie, almost cross-eyed, pleading yet angry look. We felt that there was a demonic element at work. With her permission, I cast out the demon (bound, rebuked, and cast it out in Jesus's name). The woman then grabbed me, hugging me uncomfortably while still squeezing my hand. As I repeated the name of Jesus over and over she began to relax and then straightened up. She looked rested, and her eyes were soft and lovingly relaxed.

I found an interpreter and proceeded to minister inner healing from childhood abuse, walking her through the forgiveness of her mother and anger at God. I assured her that she was not responsible for her mother's death from cancer. After suggesting additional inner healing and counseling, I reiterated God's love and acceptance of her as a child and now as an adult. She told me that when I moved her hair out of her face (actually to see deliverance progress), it reminded her of how her mother used to stroke her hair when she was being nice. I reminded her that her mother did love her, even if she couldn't always show it.

Robbie
Global Awakening mission trip to Ukraine

Cloudiness in Right Eye; Forgiveness; Witchcraft/Idolatry

A woman approached me and asked me to pray for her right eye. The eye was cloudy, and she said everything looked cloudy through it. She said her condition had been diagnosed two different ways by two different doctors. I could see for myself that her eye was cloudy. However, she felt certain there was a mass in it and that it had a spiritual cause. In the interview, it was discovered that she and her whole family had been involved in witchcraft, including her husband, but she and her husband were now Christians. She renounced the spirit of witchcraft and its power, and bondages were broken off. She forgave her relatives who had brought the spirit of witchcraft into the family. She forgave her family members for their idolatry. I commanded the spirit of witchcraft and the spirit of idolatry to leave. Then I commanded her eye to be healed in the name of Jesus. I prayed that the Holy Spirit would come with power to heal her. After a few minutes of prayer, I removed my hand from her eye. I asked if it was better, and she replied that it was. I asked what percentage of improvement she was experiencing, and she said 80 percent. I was absolutely thrilled!! I noticed the pupil of her eye was no longer cloudy. Thank You, Jesus! We all gave thanks—the woman, the interpreter, and me.

Tim

Pastor

Global Awakening mission trip to Brazil

Cutting; Suicide

Dear Randy,

This letter is a little late in coming, but it documents a miracle that took place at one of your healing schools. I'll start by giving you the background. First, it is important to know that because of the wording you used when you gave the word of knowledge, I have been an elder in the church for over twenty years. For reasons I won't go into, I stepped down from being an elder in the spring of 2003. We had irreconcilable differences with the pastor of our church. In order not to hurt any of the congregation, our plan was to step down from leadership in 2003 and then leave the church in 2004. When I attended your healing school, I was pretty much in a limbo state in terms of ministry.

Second, you must get a picture of my daughter. She was a senior attending college. Her first three years of school she had played varsity basketball, but this year, because of her curriculum load, she was not able to play. Actually, it was more than that. She had been accosted and harassed by the basketball coach, involving sexual innuendos. When her senior year started and she wasn't playing basketball, there were all sorts of accusations being thrown around that lead to the resignation of the coach. After his resignation, things got very rough for my daughter. The coach had been a winning coach, and many were angry that he was gone. My daughter began to get nasty notes from students and fans saying it was all her fault that he had resigned. It was more than she could handle, and she started slashing herself. She would cut her wrist and arms on a regular basis. She struggled with thoughts of suicide many times. When basketball season started, it pushed her over the edge, and she tried to kill herself and wound up in the psych ward for four days. Obviously, her mother and I were having a terrible time. We couldn't get the support we needed from the church because of what we were going through. We tried to help our girl, but it didn't seem to be working.

It was then that I happened to attend Randy's healing school. It was a great experience, but the last night you gave a strange word of knowledge. I could tell you were having trouble getting it out. You finally said, "There is a Bible teacher here who has a very sick daughter. You need to come and claim her healing." Well, that was me, and I did. It was difficult because by the time I got up front, the "free for all" prayer had already begun, but somehow I was able to make it over to you. You prayed and broke the demonic stronghold over our family.

I went home two days later, and the following day I called our daughter and told her I had some really good news for her and wanted to drive up that day and take her to dinner. At dinner I told her the whole story. We then prayed, and I released over her the healing you had declared—that it was over. She immediately started doing better. She was on some very heavy meds that she gradually started backing off of. She graduated with her class. One requirement of graduation was to engage in a cross-cultural experience. We were able to arrange for her to spend a month in the Philippines working with friends who run a private Christian school.

I am happy to report that our daughter is doing well now, teaching special education.

Randy, when we look back at this, we know it was a miracle that came as a word of knowledge from you. We really want to thank you, but most of all we want to thank our wonderful God, who goes to incredible extremes to save us.

Frank
Global Awakening School of Healing

Damaged Emotions; Lying; Sexual Sin; Salvation

I ministered to a woman requesting healing prayer who was upset that for all the times she had received prayer, she hadn't been healed. She not only had no faith for her healing; she had less than no faith. She was obstinate with the translator, and we found out that she wasn't saved. Her life was filled with many vices: cigarettes, lying, fornication, etc. With the interpreter's help, I explained the coming Judgment, and then the Gospel, and then we led her to Christ. We then prayed for a cleansing, and she proceeded to renounce several sins with many tears. We prayed for the Holy Spirit to heal her broken/damaged emotions and for the Spirit to fill her. She fell back to the floor (we gently laid her down), and her eyelids were quickly fluttering. She told us that she felt enormous peace and the presence of God. If she comes back for healing prayer, we'll gladly pray for her healing, as we ran out of time.

Michael

Pastor

Global Awakening mission trip to Brazil

Deafness in Both Ears; Macumba, Witchcraft, Black Magic, and White Magic

A man had been mostly deaf in both ears since he was a young child. He told us he heard a lot of clutter in his head. I found out that his mother had been in a Macumba cult when he was young. I had him break the curses of Macumba, witchcraft, black magic, and white magic, and then we cast out those spirits, along with the deafness. He could hear everything almost instantly. I had the interpreter step back to test his hearing. We were in the midst of a crowd, and he said it was too loud. His was the second healing of deafness on this trip that was directly related to Macumba.

Norman

Global Awakening mission trip to Brazil

Deafness; Curse; Spiritism

A woman came to my prayer line and asked for me to pray for her right ear. She had been deaf in that ear since she was nine years old. I interviewed her to find out why she was deaf, and she said that a childhood disease had caused swelling in her ear. I asked whether there was spiritist influence, and she told me that while she was ill and lying in bed, she could hear her neighbor chanting (she was a spiritist). We broke the power of any curse on her and then began to pray for her ear. We prayed, "More power, more anointing," which was the extent of my vast foreign language skills, but nothing happened at first. We prayed more, and she felt heat in her ears. She shook violently and leaned her head to the right and was shaking her head like she was trying to get something out of her ear. We stopped and checked her ear. She listened, smiled, and then screamed cheers and fell to the ground, crying like a baby. She went to her pastor to give a testimony later on.

John
Global Awakening mission trip to Brazil

Depression; Witchcraft

A woman came up for prayer for deliverance from depression. She said that she cried all the time, was always sad, and had pain all over her body. As we began casting out the spirit of depression, she slowly fell over backward like a board, and then she began arching her back and screaming as the demons manifested themselves. As we cast out the demons, she snapped back to normal, and we dug deeper into her life and began breaking curses and all the spirits of witchcraft in which she had been involved. After several manifestations, she renounced all curses, blessed the people she had cursed, and was totally delivered and began singing praises to God!

Crystal
Global Awakening Youth Power Invasion
trip to Curitiba, Brazil

Eye Pressure; Chest Pain; Thyroid Disorder; Spirit of Discouragement; Spiritism, Satanism

The service opened with a time for words of knowledge. I felt pressure around my left eye and gave the word. Immediately a man raised his hand. When I interviewed him, he told me he was a missionary in Spain. The eye problem started after a local satanist cursed him. We prayed and broke the curse, and immediately he felt the pressure relieved. It had affected his ability to focus, and he testified that he could now see clearly. We also prayed for pressure in the heart area of his chest. This too left almost immediately. The power level was very high! After this, I immediately prayed for another woman who had pressure and inflammation in her right eye. Her vision was impaired. She could not read a banner on the wall. We asked for the Holy Spirit to come, and immediately He did. She had practiced spiritism for ten years. We prayed a prayer of renunciation and again prayed for her eye. Immediately, she felt fire in her eye. The pressure and burning she had felt prior to the meeting left instantly. She read the banner on the wall and was so happy! I also prayed for a woman with a thyroid condition, which caused enlarged eyes and loss of vision. When we asked the Holy Spirit to come, waves of power went through her as she went down. She began to weep as the Holy Spirit moved. She confessed great sadness because she had had much prayer and yet the condition had remained. Also, she has a ministry to children in the poor area and was discouraged and had stopped praying for a deaf girl because nothing had happened. I shared testimonies of healings I had seen, and she laughed for ten minutes as God removed the sadness and encouraged her. Then fire hit her eyes, and she felt the pressure go; and she could see clearly again!

Dennis
Global Awakening mission trip to Brazil

Fear; Spirit of Death; Lying Spirit

A woman came forward asking for prayer to be set free from fear. Her mom had died of cancer, and the enemy was telling her that she was going to die from cancer also. We explained that it was a lie, and she repented for believing it and for her fear. We cast out the spirit of fear and death and the lying spirit, and joy came into her. I prophesied that she would be used of God for healing, and she fell down weeping. She said through her sobs, "I know. I can feel that God is calling me into healing, and other people have prophesied the same thing."

Stacy

Missionary

Global Awakening mission trip to Ukraine

Generational Sin—Witchcraft; Sexual Sin/Prostitution; Forgiveness

The following is an example of generational sin opening doors in children. I was in Madrid, Spain, in 2004, ministering at a facility for drug addicts and prostitutes. During the praise and worship portion of the service, a fourteen-year-old girl named Janilda fell to the floor and manifested. She exhibited tormented behaviors by banging her head and pulling her hair. Three team members helped me pick her up (with her mother's permission) and take her to a quiet room. Her mother served as our translator. We took authority and spoke peace to the girl. I asked the mother if we could perform deliverance ministry on her daughter. She begged us to do so, as she was extremely distressed over her daughter's condition. The young girl was severely tormented and often unable to speak. The mother indicated that the torment had been terrible for a long time.

I interviewed the mother, suspecting generational sin. I began the process of explaining generational sin and forgiveness. The mother began to weep while I was speaking to her. I took her aside and pressed her for the truth; however, we hit a wall. The demonic spirit was still strong and authorized to be present. Finally, the mother began to open up. She said that she had been a Christian for eight years. However, she stated that Janilda had been born out of wedlock and that her father (Janilda's grandfather) had forced the mother and her two sisters into prostitution. Moreover the grandmother was involved in witchcraft. The mother confessed, repented, and forgave her father, mother, and herself. This broke the authorization of the generational curse.

After I took authority over the witchcraft, prostitution, immorality, and rejection, Janilda became peaceful—but not totally free. Then I had Janilda confess Jesus as her Lord and Savior and renounce witchcraft, an orphan spirit, rejection, and abandonment. Subsequently, the demonic presence left. When she prayed to receive the Holy Spirit, it was glorious! She and her mother hugged and cried in each other's arms. Team member Phil Walls prayed the father's blessing over her and gave her twenty dollars, as it was Janilda's spiritual birthday! She was a new creature in Christ Jesus, and we gave Him the victory!

Testimony from Tom Hauser's *Breaking Free*

Headache; Abdominal Pain

This mission trip was truly a faith builder for me. I am the pastor of a relatively small mainline denominational church. Occasionally, I see a few souls saved and periodically a healing. I came on this trip in need of, and prepared to experience, the power of the Holy Spirit at work, and I did! Friday morning worship was the kick-off for me. It was the beginning of operating in the Spirit at a level I had never consistently experienced before. At an early morning expatriate service, the worship was both intense and sincere. We were among the poorest and lowest in the society. Later in the morning, we went to another expatriate church, where the hunger for God and the expectation that He would give the worshipers more of Himself was simply overwhelming. Following the message, people came forward. They just kept coming and coming. Some sought the baptism of the Holy Spirit; others wanted more of whatever the Lord wanted to give them. Still others simply wanted to abandon themselves to Him. As I lay hands on them, they would almost immediately fall down under the influence of the Spirit.

I had never experienced ministry that was so easy or so much fun. That evening, ministry continued to flow through us with ease. One man's healing I called the "Pepto-Bismol miracle." He had a headache above one eye and severe abdominal pain. One short prayer—and the headache was gone. The second prayer required more. I prayed in the name of Jesus, then asked him how he was feeling. He replied that the pain had moved lower. I prayed that it would move down and out. Then, in a word of knowledge, I told him, "I sense you will go to the bathroom within thirty minutes." Approximately a half hour later, his face beaming, he came to shake my hand and give thanks for his healing!

Dave
Pastor
Global Awakening mission trip to the Middle East

Headaches; Satanism/Witchcraft

A Brazilian lady came for prayer, and fortunately we had a translator. She told me that some time ago, she had a kidney tumor. The doctors thought that she would only live for two more weeks or so. God healed her, and she became a Christian. Then she told me that she had bad headaches and every time she would go to sleep in the middle of the night, she would wake up and the headache would be really bad. I started to pray for her and asked if she had emotional problems. She said yes because her husband and mother-in-law practiced witchcraft and were satanists. She was worried because none of her children and her family go to church. Because I am a teacher for the ten-step deliverance model, it was time for me to practice. It was obviously a generational curse or curse in the family. I led her in renunciation, breaking the bondage, then prayed a prayer of blessing that she would be filled with the Holy Spirit. She started dancing, jumping, and laughing! She was overjoyed, and her headache was gone! She was so touched by God. It was my first time ministering deliverance with this particular ten-step model, and it was so great to see how God first filled me and then used me to fill His other children! God's ways are higher than ours, and if we obey and are willing, He will use us to expand His Kingdom!

Winnie
Global Awakening mission trip to Brazil

Infertility; Soul Ties

I prayed with a young woman who had come to the meeting from another city because she believed Jesus was going to heal her. She was suffering from severe pain across the lower abdomen and had not been menstruating for four years. She was on medication from the doctor. I asked the Holy Spirit to come, and she immediately fell down under the anointing. The pain became even more severe. I prayed to break off any curses that had been put on her and to cancel the power of anything that had come down the generation lines to her. I spoke health and healing into her reproductive system. She reported that the pain was 70 percent better. I asked whether she had had sexual relations before she was married. She said yes but she had asked for forgiveness. I broke the soul tie between her and the man she had been with and prayed for healing, commanding the pain to go. She stood up praising Jesus and glowing with the most beautiful smile and said she was completely free from pain!

Jan Harvey
Homemaker
Global Awakening mission trip to Brazil

Intestinal Problems

A young woman in her mid-twenties had intestinal problems and was unable to work. Her mother told us that she (the daughter) volunteered at the church. Another team member and I prayed for deliverance, and eventually the demonic strongholds were broken and she was released.

The power of God came upon her, causing her to fall to the floor, where she lay for some time receiving ministry. Afterwards she reported feeling 100 percent better and was all smiles. Two days later, we attended another small village church, and she was there leading worship. What a dramatic change! Total victory over satan!

Maude
English Teacher and Writer
Global Awakening mission trip to China

Lameness; Herniated Disk

Our team was ministering at a church about an hour and a half outside of the city. Those in need of physical healing were invited up for prayer. Someone approached to tell us that there was a woman in the back who needed healing, but she was not able to come up front because she couldn't walk. I took a team member, and we went back to pray for her. As we prayed, she indicated that she felt nothing. We were spoiled because others we prayed for were falling out under the Spirit and being healed rapidly. After ten minutes or so, the pain in her leg moved to a different location. We commanded the spirit of affliction to go, and it did. With her leg pain now gone, our faith surged, and we prayed for the herniated disk in her back. Within just a few moments she was able to stand and then walk for the first time in months. With her husband sobbing at her side and the whole church cheering, she walked to the front to give her testimony. Praise God for He is awesome beyond words!

Carol
Portfolio Manager
Global Awakening mission trip to Brazil

Lump on Neck; Forgiveness

Kathy and I prayed for a lady with a large lump on her neck. It would go down with prayer, but then it would come back. After trying several approaches, she revealed a deep sin/wound that had tormented her for many years. She had just rededicated her life to Jesus so we helped her accept forgiveness and forgive herself. After that, the lump was gone and stayed gone.

Michelle

Scientist

Global Awakening mission trip to Brazil

Macumba; Blood Sacrifices; Sexual Sin/Prostitution; Salvation

Belém, Brazil, is known for its Macumba witchcraft and spiritualism. This testimony is from a deliverance crusade with Randy Clark and Global Awakening. There were approximately eighteen thousand people in attendance at the crusade. During one meeting a fifteen-year-old girl named Anna received Christ. Immediately after receiving Jesus as her personal Savior, she began to manifest with violent convulsions and vomit blood. Eight members of my church surrounded me as I led an "on the job training" deliverance session. A Portuguese interpreter was also present, as none on the team could speak the language and Anna couldn't speak English.

Through an interpreter we learned that Anna was a prostitute and that her mother was a Macumba witch. Anna had been involved in Macumba rituals and blood sacrifices. We then knew that this demonic authorization was likely from generational witchcraft and sexual sin. Anna wanted to be free from the demonic influence over her life, and we were determined to see her completely set free.

Anna carried many demons. Normally in a situation such as hers, more time would have been spent on forgiveness and confession to weaken the authorization before expelling trespassers. This proved difficult because a demonic spirit kept trying to control her voice. One team member, Mark, held Anna's head as I spoke to the translator. Suddenly the demon began to speak in perfect English to Mark: "I am going to kill her and you when I come out!" Speaking with authority, I told the spirit that it was a liar and that it would come out of Anna. As we spoke in tongues, the spirit again spoke in English: "It is very hot in here," it said. I replied, "Good!" The team continued to speak in tongues. This went on for over two hours. Finally, the spirit said, "I am leaving," and it left. Anna regained a clear conscience, spoke in her native Portuguese, and indicated through our interpreter that the torment was gone.

The following day, Anna was barely recognizable. She was peaceful, full of joy, and happy to be free.

Testimony from Tom Hauser's *Breaking Free*

Macumba; Degenerative Neurological Disease; Lameness

A lady came for prayer. For ten years she had suffered from a degenerative neurological disease and had not walked unaided for over a year. I checked for issues that might have precipitated this condition and found out that her husband was in a Macumba cult, but she was not. With the blood of Jesus, I broke off the curses from Macumba (see Gal. 3:13). Then I laid my hands on her head. I could feel the heat of the anointing in my hands, and when I asked her how she felt, she said her feet were burning up. I told her God's healing anointing was going through her head down to her feet for a complete healing. After a few minutes, she said she felt completely better with no pain at all. She attempted to walk and walked across the church for the first time in a year without any assistance. She felt as if she had to learn to walk again so we prayed for her legs and feet. She walked a few more steps and said that her legs felt stronger. Praise the Lord!

Neil
Global Awakening mission trip to Rio de Janeiro, Brazil

Macumba; Lameness; Arm and Leg Length Discrepancies; Spirit of Abandonment; Forgiveness

A teenage girl who could not walk properly for twelve years and couldn't run at all came for prayer. She had been praying and fasting for healing and felt that Macumba, practiced by her grandfather, was the cause of her difficulties. We prayed for deliverance and then started praying for healing for her legs. She felt tingling in them and was able to walk a little better, but they were still tingling and aching. Then a Brazilian came and said he had a word of knowledge that her legs would be healed. We checked to see if one side of her body was longer than the other. When we tested her arms, we found one was shorter. As we prayed that the shorter arm would grow, we saw it lengthen and had to shout "Stop!" because it was growing so fast we could see it would soon be longer than the other. She said she felt it grow. I gave her a hug! We then checked her legs and found one longer than the other. Another Brazilian came over and told us that we needed to ask her about her relationship with her parents. Her father had abandoned her, and she did not get on well with her mother. Knowing this, we began to pray for Jesus to come and heal her broken heart. She wept loudly for quite some time as the deep pain surfaced and Jesus healed her emotions. Then she forgave her parents. We then prayed again for her legs and commanded the shorter one to grow. When it looked as though they were about the same length, she tried walking again and then she was able to run!

Jackie
Retired University Lecturer
Global Awakening mission trip to Brazil

64

Macumba; Paralysis; Salvation

At one of the meetings, I prayed for a man in a wheelchair. He was paralyzed due to a diving accident. First, I led him in a salvation prayer. When he said the name "Jesus," a demon manifested. Along with the pastor, my interpreter, and the lady who brought him, we took him to the pastor's office to minister deliverance. He had so many demons. Every time we would lead him in prayer to renounce an activity associated with Macumba, the demons would take over. We spent over two and half hours with him. He prayed several different prayers renouncing demonic activity in his life. I would put my hands up to block the view of the demons so he could concentrate and finish what he was praying. I would see his eyes following the demons as they flew around the room trying to come back into him. We told him that the devil can only have control of what we allow him to control. It was a pretty intense deliverance, but he was totally delivered!

Violet
Global Awakening mission trip to Brazil

Macumba; Strokes; Lameness

An eleven-year-old boy was sitting in a chair in the middle of the arena. With tears in their eyes, his mother and father said he had just had his third stroke one month ago. The boy said he came to be healed and he was not leaving until he could walk! Such faith from an eleven-year-old! His legs were like putty, and he could only shuffle for a few minutes if someone held him up from behind. I asked him to stand, and with no hesitation, he stood up. I held him from the front and sort of dragged him about ten feet. Then I wrapped the "Spencer blessing" around him (the Spencer blessing is my four-year-old granddaughter's cloud blanket that she asked me to bring to bless the children). I said, "Walk in the name of Jesus," then turned him around, took only his fingertips, and told him he would not fall, that Jesus had him. He walked clear across the stadium floor with people screaming, "Hallelujah! Gloria!" the whole way. He was very, very, very happy. Pastor Tom Hauser came over and sealed what had taken place, prayed for the family, and asked them to repent of sins and clear their home of any idols or Macumba. They agreed, and although they lived forty miles away, they said they would be back the following night. Our God is an awesome God!

Cookie

Global Awakening mission trip to Brazil

Nodes on Neck; Afflicting Spirit

The second night at the gym, a man approached me with a girl clinging to his pant leg. He showed me her neck, which had two protruding nodes halfway between her ear and shoulder. I told the girl my name and asked her name and age. She said, "Priscilla, seven." Her father gave me more information in Portuguese. Without the benefit of a translator, I at least understood that they had previously been to a doctor. Using hand signals I indicated that we would pray to "Doctor Jesus." I put my hand on the nodes and prayed briefly. There was no change. I motioned to the girl and her father that all of us were going to pray. We did so, and moments later, the nodes disappeared. The girl had a bright smile and pulled on her dad as if to say, "OK, let's go!" Her dad and I were standing, saying, "Gloria, Aleluya!" when she suddenly looked up and, pointing to the side of her face, said, "Oh! Aqui!" A single node had suddenly appeared there. I motioned to a translator to join us and explained what we had done up to that point. I had him tell the girl and her father what I had just learned through Randy's course on healing—that if a problem changes location after prayer it may be due to an afflicting spirit. I then told the translator and the father that we would all speak with the authority of Jesus to command the afflicting sprit to leave and never return. We did so. Priscilla looked up happily and said, "It's gone," and it was!

Marie
Registered Nurse and Missionary in Nicaragua
Global Awakening mission trip to Vitória, Brazil

Pain in Joints; Osteoporosis; Vision Loss; Addiction

One evening, I received a word of knowledge that there were several men and women over sixty-five years of age who were suffering from osteoporosis and vision issues. Throughout the evening, about half a dozen older people came up for prayer. One woman was suffering from pain in all of her joints. After deliverance and prayers for healing, she said that she felt young again and had no pain. She then went home to retrieve some family photos and returned and stood in line for four hours to have me pray for her family members in the photos. Two of them were saved; three were unsaved and battled addictions. We prayed for those who were not yet saved and for her to have the courage to talk to them about Jesus. She was weeping and thanking God for the chance to minister to her family and said she still felt 100 percent healed of pain from osteoporosis.

John
Administrative Pastor
Global Awakening mission trip to Brazil

Parkinson's Disease; Occult

A lady came for prayer for Parkinson's disease. Her daughter was concerned for her mother's health and also concerned because her mother had many idols in her home. Feeling a strong anointing, I placed my hands on the mother's head and the power of God came upon her. She reported that she felt heat flowing through her body. As the healing anointing flowed, I proceeded to pray, telling her that Jesus was her healer and the author and finisher of her faith, and therefore she needed to focus on Jesus and make sure that all idols were out of the way. We had her remove her necklace with Mary on it, and the anointing touched her. Her daughter then said she (the daughter) had participated in the occult when she was younger. As we ministered deliverance to the daughter, she began to cough and was set free. Her face was glowing with peace. We asked her mother to check her hand tremors. She extended her hands with no tremors. Mother and daughter were both healed!

Neil
Global Awakening mission trip to Rio de Janeiro, Brazil

Post-Traumatic Stress Disorder; Insomnia

I asked Mike Hutchings to pray for me for healing from the chronic insomnia from which I have suffered ever since my husband lost his job in 2011. I am a career nurse of over thirty-five years, and I've seen too much. I also experienced trauma in my childhood. I was unaware that the root issue was a wound in my soul. I have not been able to sleep in the same bed with my husband in ten years. I felt too much "fight or flight," and any noise would disturb me. When Mike prayed for me, I was very uncomfortable. I didn't like that he asked me to keep looking at his eyes because when I did, I sensed all the shame that has haunted me. I felt ashamed that I could not trust God more. Mike held my wrists, and I immediately felt combative. He sensed what was going on and said, "Gina, you are waiting for the other shoe to drop? God says it's not going to drop anymore." That phrase is what I have said to myself many times. Mike prayed powerfully, and I experienced God's presence in such a unique way. A heavy sense of peace came upon me. Physically, the peace was so heavy I ended up on the floor! Since I've been home, I've slept amazingly well. I'm 75–80 percent better. I have such a heaviness of deep slumber during the night and amazing peace too. In fact, I've been going to bed early because I have so much sleep to catch up on. During the day, I have energy instead of dragging through, hoping it will end soon. I am starting to thrive instead of just survive. Thank You, Jesus; and thank you, Mike; and thank you, Global Awakening!

Gina

Post-Traumatic Stress Disorder; Child Abuse; Witchcraft

My friend, Allison and I were attending a Global Awakening Kingdom Foundations school in Olena, New York. Allison is a veteran who joined the military when she was seventeen and served for ten years. She worked in special ops and was rated at 100 percent disability with PTSD. I have suffered with psychological problems since I was three years old. I was told I would never been cured. I was a victim of child abuse, witchcraft, and sorcery. My stepmother was from Cali, Colombia, and she would practice voodoo. I had been praying for deliverance for years. I had moments where I felt God's presence, but I couldn't get free. As of yesterday, I am 100 percent delivered! I haven't needed my meds, I can sleep, I am happy, I don't have anxiety, and I don't have fear about being around people. I have my life back! And my faith in God has been restored. Coping with pain makes you want to stand on your own two feet instead of letting God take the lead. I thought I needed to be strong so I could survive, but you cannot fix your brokenness in your own power. You have to let Jesus help you. You have to let go of control and become vulnerable. When I was able to trust Jesus and let go, I received my healing and deliverance. I was triggered left and right in the PTSD seminar, but I didn't leave because I needed my healing. When I ran out to get my breath, one of the ladies, Lori, ran out after me. She knew what was going on. She sat there and talked to me. It was a divine appointment, and I received divine healing. Jesus loves us so much.

Ritual Abuse; Genetic Illness; Bone Marrow Transplant

On the second night of the conference, I mentioned something to one of the team members about a genetic illness of which I am a carrier and for which my older son has had a bone marrow transplant. This team member took the three of us out with a couple of other team members and started to ask lots of questions—all the right questions; he has great discernment. I told him about being ritually abused when I was a child. What followed was three hours of amazing deliverance. It was pretty horrible but very powerful. At one point, two other team members joined us. Five members of Global Awakening's wonderful team poured their love and gifts into us. My sons stayed with me the whole time (they are sixteen and thirteen years old) and even discerned a couple of things that needed to be dealt with. The whole experience was very definitely a God appointment.

I have had prayer for all sorts of abuse and have been trained in deliverance and inner healing myself. However, I was blown away by what God did and by the love and support of the team. I experienced a whole new dimension to ministry and have never felt so lovingly surrounded and valued. The difference it made was apparent straightaway and is getting more so each day. On the last night I was able to receive from God in a way I never have before.

The whole conference was a huge blessing. My boys had lots of prayer and soaked up everything Randy and Gary had to say. Joe, the younger one, received lots of healing. He's been unwell for over a year. They were incredibly impacted by Jamie and want to be like him—totally sold out on God and spreading His truth and love in power. They both want to go to Brazil. I'm not sure if that can happen this year, but if not, they are determined to go next year. The time at the conference was life changing for all of us. We are wondering where we go from here. We are all absolutely sure that God has work for us, and we can't wait to walk into it. Thank you for all the love and effort that goes into Global Awakening. I hope someday we can thank you personally.

Jane, John, and Joe

Global Awakening conference in England

Scoliosis

A fifteen-year-old boy born with scoliosis came to me for prayer. All of his ribs on one side of his chest were twisted and deformed, and his back was out of alignment. One leg was five centimeters shorter than the other. There were other problems associated with the scoliosis that I didn't fully understand because my translators went to pray for someone else. The boy thought a curse had come upon him through his father's spiritual practices. I declared over him that Jesus broke every curse on the cross. Then I commanded all effects of the curse to be reversed and every bone and joint in his body to be made perfect. He immediately began to twist and turn and go into the strangest contortions I have ever seen. Many of the movements looked completely impossible. His arms looked like they were going to come out of their sockets. His face looked like he was in pain, but he was laughing at the same time. He soon fell to the floor and continued the same wild movements. After another several minutes of prayer, I asked him to check his body. He said his ribs were in perfect position and his hip had moved into place. One leg was still a little short so I commanded it to grow, and in a few seconds it was exactly the right length. The boy found a doctor at the meeting who checked his spine and confirmed that everything was aligned! Hallelujah!

Gary

Construction Estimator

Global Awakening mission trip to Brazil

Skull Malformation; Crossed Eyes

A woman brought her baby boy of about six months of age for healing prayer. He was born with brain damage. A ridge ran down the center of his skull that was about one-fourth of an inch high in the front and that diminished toward the back of the head. Both of his eyes were crossed. I began to pray, and as I did, a feeling of defeat started coming into my mind. I had to remind myself that it is God that does the healing and that He was allowing me to participate. I prayed for a long time and was just about to lose hope. The woman had been holding her baby face up against her body with his head in her hand and the body supported by her arm. I had seen no change up to this point. Suddenly, the boy's head jerked forward, and projectile vomit flew out of his mouth onto the ground. His head came back, and I saw his eyes straighten and focus. When I looked, I noticed that at the top of his head the ridge was gone. He had a little smile on his face as he moved his eyes, checking out everything around him. His mother and grandmother had tears in their eyes and joy on their faces. I began to realize that I had just watched a demon get evicted!

Gary
Retired
Global Awakening mission trip to Brazil

Sexual Sin/Soul Ties; Emotional Pain

A woman named Elizabeth came to Tuesday night's meeting seeking relief from emotional pain, which she said originated from early sexual relations. As Randy began speaking of God's willingness to heal us, Elizabeth said she felt heat throughout her body. She sensed the presence of someone near her and turned to see who it was, but nobody was there. I said, "Jesus, is that You?" Suddenly, she said that she saw a bright light and felt everything lifting off of her. Then she felt an electric shock course through her body. As Randy explained the anointing of the Holy Spirit, often evidenced by that feeling of electricity, she fell out in the Spirit. Later that night, she said she felt as light as a feather and that all the emotional torment was gone.

Norman
Global Awakening mission trip to Europe

Spirits of Death and Murder; Abortions; Back Pain; Forgiveness; Guilt and Shame

I prayed for a lady who wanted to be closer to the Lord. She had a bad dream about a cockroach eating a butterfly, which we took to mean something dirty or unclean was blocking Jesus from transforming her life. She also had back pain. She said it began sixteen years ago when she had an abortion. It turned out she had had at least four abortions. She had asked for God's forgiveness, but when she forgave herself, she began to improve. We canceled spirits of murder and death and broke their power. Then she felt strangled. With the help of another team member we asked her to look to Jesus on the cross and give Him all her guilt and shame. When we asked what Jesus did, she said, "He took it, and He has a big smile on His face." We asked the Holy Spirit to fill her. When I asked about her back pain, she said there was only a little bit. We asked Jesus to heal that, which He did immediately. She was completely healed and delivered. Thank You, Jesus!

Kris
Retired Teacher
Global Awakening mission trip to Ukraine

Spirits of Death and Murder; Abuse; Spirit of Rejection; Forgiveness; Emotional Healing

A woman approached me requesting prayer for her feet. She had been injured several years ago in an automobile accident. I prayed several times without much result. I was seeking the Lord about how to pray, and then I began to talk with her about her relationship with the Lord. She was able to open up and told me that her husband had abused her when she was very young and had tried to kill her. He had been lost at sea and never found. However, before his death she had two children, whom he also abused. As she shared about her life, she talked as though she were talking about someone else—without emotions or feelings. I began to lead her in prayers of forgiveness, renouncing rejection, the spirit of murder, and several other things. As we prayed, tears began to flow down her cheeks. We were able to close doors to the enemy and open doors of love, forgiveness, and acceptance, and I could see change taking place in her. God really began a process of inner healing for her that night.

Cathy
Project Manager
Global Awakening mission trip to Auckland, New Zealand

Spirit of Depression

I had a word of knowledge for "depression." A woman who had been suffering from depression because of the loss of a child two years ago came for prayer. We cast out the spirits of depression, despondency, discouragement, hopelessness, heaviness, gloom, burden, and death. She felt freedom as the depression left. Then we proceeded to explain to her how to keep her healing, telling her that when she thinks about her child and dwells on it, the depression could return—unless she keeps an awareness of the need to constantly turn her thoughts toward the Lord and to put on the garment of praise for the spirit of heaviness. She came depressed and left happy and smiling. Praise God!

Norman
Retired
Global Awakening mission trip to Spain,
England, and Switzerland

Spirit of Rejection

Someone came to me and asked me to help pray for a lady who felt like she had a demon. I was nervous because I had never prayed for such a thing before, but I did it. We started praying for her, and she was immediately knocked to the ground. After a while, she got up and said she felt so much better. Someone suggested I give her a hug, so I did, and she immediately began to weep. I broke the spirit of rejection over her life and told her that Jesus loved her, and she began to scream and cry. After about five minutes, I let her go, and she told the translators that she had been praying to God for someone to come and hug her and show her love and that now she felt an emotional healing go through her body. Glory to God!

Christa
Global Awakening mission trip to Brazil

Spirit of Rejection; Pain in Arm; Forgiveness

I was given a word of knowledge about pain in the left arm above the elbow. There was not an opportunity to speak the word, but later God prompted me to give it anyway! A lady immediately responded. She had had pains in her arm for four years. I felt that God told me that her condition was related to trauma and a stressful incident. It later came out that she had a painful separation. She was able to forgive her husband. We prayed, the pain left, and the Lord told me there was a spirit of rejection. I prayed, and a demon manifested, growling and clawing, but was quickly silenced and soon left. She was touched by the Holy Spirit and afterwards said that her arm was better and that a great blockage had been removed from her.

Trina
Pastor/Missionary
Global Awakening mission trip to Brazil

Suicide/Spirit of Death; Leg Length Discrepancy; Religious Spirit; Spiritism

My wife and I and an interpreter prayed for a young pastor who came to us. He said that he was separated from his wife and that he wanted to commit suicide. He also said that he had problems with his ministry and that legalism and control were very prevalent in his church. After interviewing him, we learned that he was married to a woman five years his senior and that her first husband had committed suicide. He also said that his mother-in-law, who had lived with him and his wife for some time, was involved in spiritism. She had placed a curse on her daughter's husbands. We led him through the deliverance process, and he was able to forgive his wife and mother-in-law and church family. As we prayed for him, he fell under the power of the Holy Spirit and began to curl up on the floor. The manifestations continued for some time, and then peace came over him. When he got up, he said that he felt much better and that the suicidal feelings had left. Glory to God! During the evening service, the same young man came over and tapped Bert on the shoulders and requested prayers for his left leg, which was shorter than the right one. Bert prayed for him, and much to the pastor's delight, the left leg grew out to the same length as the other leg. The interpreter was surprised. Everyone praised God and gave Him the glory for what He had done!

Bert and Hyacinth
Global Awakening mission trip to Londrina, Brazil

Uterine and Ovarian Problems; Pain; Curse

A woman asked me for prayer for problems with her uterus and ovaries and for pain in her breast. She told me that she had been healed but that the pain had come back. When I asked her if anything had happened prior to her health problems, she told me, "No." I started praying, and the Holy Spirit told me it was a curse. I asked if anyone could have done such a thing, and she confirmed it. I told her to forgive the person and to ask forgiveness from God for her anger toward this person. After she did this, I broke the curse in Jesus's name! The moment that the curse was broken, the pain left. Praise to the Father!

Pietie

Nurse

Global Awakening mission trip to Ukraine

Witchcraft; Sexual Abuse; Breast Cancer; Spirit of Death (Abortion); Spirit of Rejection; Adultery; Forgiveness; Shoulder Issues

The following occurred while in Manchester, England, on a mission outreach with Global Awakening. During one of our meetings, a woman came up to me for prayer. I discerned a spirit of death the moment I saw her. I asked her how I could pray for her. She responded by telling me of her plight with breast cancer. She indicated that she had undergone chemotherapy and had recently had a mastectomy. As soon as I began to pray for her, she manifested. She suddenly became stiff, and her hands curled up. I immediately prayed for peace, and she was then able to relax. I asked her if she would be willing to come back the next day so that we could spend focused time in a quiet setting, and she agreed. I asked her to prepare for the ministry session by making a forgiveness and confession list.

The following day, I was joined by my prayer-warrior mother and two members from my church. We quickly learned the following: Trisha had been a Christian for over ten years and was active in church ministry. She went on to give us insight into her turbulent childhood. She indicated that she never felt any love from her mother growing up. Sadly, she had been molested by an older man who babysat her as a child. She had also been molested by her older brother. Her first child had been born out of wedlock. She had four children and was married to the father of her last three.

She described how four years prior, she was very active in her church and was once asked to lead the Scripture reading for the Christmas Eve service. She expressed that during the Scripture reading, she began to feel sick. This sick feeling persisted into the next day. Around the same time, she discovered unraveled cassette tape wrapped around some bushes at her house. She explained that the local witch coven regularly curses Christians by speaking curses into a tape recorder and then stringing the tape around churches or people's houses. Trisha had not conducted spiritual warfare to combat the spiritual attack. She simply picked up the tapes and threw them away. She believed that while she was attending the Christmas Eve service, the witches had visited her home. Since then, the following situations had occurred in her life: all four of her children had been arrested, she had developed breast cancer, her husband had quit attending church and began visiting a prostitute, she had had an affair while on vacation with her mother in Turkey, and she had been asked to leave her church. She felt unloved by God and unable to worship anymore.

Trisha explained in detail her extramarital affair in Turkey. She said that her mother initiated the event, saying that it was justified by Trisha's husband's extracurricular activities. Her mother enticed the date by purchasing Trisha a gold bracelet. She had continued to wear the gold bracelet, and consequently the hand with the bracelet developed warts that no medication could remove. During the meeting, there was a word of knowledge given regarding a cursed piece of jewelry. That day, Trisha disposed of the bracelet in a church bathroom, and soon afterward the warts miraculously disappeared.

During four hours of prayer ministry using the "Destiny Model" of forgiveness and confession, spirits of rejection, selfishness, witchcraft, and death were cast out. During a manifestation, a demon spoke and said, "I don't have to leave!" I commanded the spirit to say why it didn't have to leave, and it replied, "She is used to me." Trisha then motioned as if to strangle me. The spirit said, "I am going to get you!" I rebuked the spirit and informed it that it had no authority and that it could not hurt me, or Trisha, or any of the team members. I informed it that it had to go!

Trisha began coughing a lot. We then seemed to hit a roadblock. We asked the Holy Spirit for divine insight. One of the team members suddenly developed sharp pains in her stomach. Another quickly received a word of knowledge and asked Trisha if she had ever had an abortion. She confessed and repented of the murdering spirit. Charles then asked her if she had any sexual fantasies. She agreed and confessed this as well. After her confessions, I took authority over all unclean spirits and commanded them to leave her. The spirit then spoke again: "Alright, I'll go." Immediately, Trisha became bright and clear-headed and declared, "I'm free!"

We prayed for her to be filled with the Holy Spirit, placed the full armor of the Lord on her, and spoke a Mother and Father's Blessing over her. She was filled with such joy. Together we raised our hands, and she was ecstatic because previously she had been unable to raise her hands above her shoulders. Her shoulders were instantly healed. God is awesome!

Testimony from Tom Hauser's *Breaking Free*

Witchcraft; Torment

A woman whom I will call Sally, a church intercessor, came to me asking for prayer. She also informed me that when she tried to pray in the Spirit, she would curse violently. She had great animosity toward her husband. Sally had been a Christian for nearly twenty years. She was a mother of three, married, and a university professor with a PhD in nursing. She was not only a brilliant individual, but she also radiated a sunny personality. She was active in church and was a faithful intercessor. She was well read and had studied many books on true intimacy with the Lord. By all outward appearances, she seemed perfectly fine. I suggested a pre-prayer interview. The pre-interview helps me assess each person's needs and true desire for prayer ministry.

Sally hesitantly came in for her pre-prayer interview—she was developing cold feet. Only after hearing several life-changing testimonials from others did she change her mind and decide to continue with ministry time. I explained the "Destiny Model" process to her, then asked her specific questions. Her answers gave me immediate insight into her situation. Her husband was not a Christian and wasn't supportive of her faith. She was from a country known for its anti-Christian beliefs. For many years, she had received secular counseling, spending thousands of dollars seeking answers for her anger toward her husband. She experienced tormenting thoughts that caused her great anxiety and rage. However, her highly educated logic could not free her from this anguish. I briefly prayed with her and scheduled her prayer ministry appointment.

Two weeks later, with four to five hours set aside for uninterrupted ministry time, I, along with my ministry partner, met with Sally. She seemed to be backstroking as she informed us that she felt like she no longer needed prayer ministry. She said that after receiving prayer during the pre-interview, she was no longer tormented and that her

husband was doing wonderfully. In fact, he was now serving her breakfast in bed! I suspected that the demonic influences had taken cover for
a strategic advantage. I mentioned that since the three of us were there
and scheduled for ministry, why not follow through? Sally agreed.

She began by sharing her list of forgiveness items and then commenced with the confession process. Soon the Holy Spirit brought forth
a revelation through an illustration by my ministry partner and a word
of knowledge from me. My partner saw a burlap bag full of black seeds
of a long-ago time in history—not a modern-day image. Simultaneously,
I heard in my spirit "generational witchcraft." After sharing this knowledge with Sally, she agreed that she was aware of previous ancestral
witchcraft. She told us that her mother had been a medium and that
she had consulted psychics with her mother even after becoming a
Christian. However, she indicated that it had occurred several years
prior and that she had already asked for forgiveness of generational
witchcraft and her involvement with psychics. I pressed ahead and
asked her if she would be willing to renounce these things once again.
Even though she felt that she had previously confessed those matters
and considered them history and irrelevant, she consented to renouncing her family and ancestral involvement in witchcraft.

As soon as Sally spoke the words, "I renounce generational..." she arose,
glared at me, and started to grab me. I was forced to restrain her to protect
myself. She began speaking in a deep male voice: "She is mine. I am high
level, and you can't have her." I spoke back with authority: "I know someone higher than you. His name is Jesus, and in His name I have authority
over you. You can't have her. She has confessed, and you're a trespasser!"
The demonic spirit began to whine, "Where will I go?" I commanded, "Go
to the dry places created by Jesus for you." The spirit then said, "Okay" and
left her. Finally, Sally, deeply embarrassed, looked at me and began to apologize profusely for the episode that had just taken place.

Soon after, she presented the church with a sizable donation. She expressed that she had wasted years and countless dollars in secular therapy and that the four hours spent in our prayer ministry session was extremely cost effective! Sally could not contain her gratitude and joy over her deliverance. She stood before the church and proclaimed her testimony of God's supernatural healing power. Today, she no longer suffers from torment. She continues to teach at the university and heads a successful Sunday school program.

Her witness serves as a powerful testimony of the stark reality of the demonic realm and the doors that can be opened by our ancestors. Sin can also give these dark influences authorization by our own rebellion. Praise Jesus. He is our Healer, our Deliverer, and our Savior!

Testimony from Tom Hauser's *Breaking Free*

Digestive System

The DIGESTIVE SYSTEM receives (digests and absorbs) food and eliminates waste. The reception of food involves chewing (with one's jaws and teeth), swallowing, and salivary gland secretion. Digestion takes place in the stomach and the duodenum. Absorption takes place in the jejunum, the ileum, and the large intestine. Evacuation happens via the rectum, the anal canal, and the anus. Accessory digestive organs are the liver, the pancreas, and the peritoneum.

I am the living bread that came down from heaven.
Whoever eats this bread will live forever. This bread is
My flesh, which I will give for the life of the world.
—JOHN 6:51

Acid Reflux; Stomach Pain

A man named Paulo approached me for prayer, and I could see by his face that he was in intense pain and desperate for God to heal him. He had stomach pain with a burning sensation that started in his stomach and went up his esophagus. As best as I could make out, it was something like acid reflux. He had suffered from this problem and had been treated by doctors for ten years. At one time, he was treated almost every day for two years. The sickness would be helped at times but always came back. As I started praying for him, the Holy Ghost led me to pray in tongues. As I did, the Holy Spirit came over him, and he began to stagger and shake violently, ending up on the floor, where he stayed for a long time. I moved down the line to pray for the next man. When I saw Paulo later, I asked him how he was doing. He told me he was healed, and God's peace was evident on his face.

John Brock
General Contractor
Global Awakening mission trip to Brazil

Broken Jaw

Our team was at a church in São Paulo, Brazil. As ministry time began, the team lined up across the front of the church. People began queuing up in front of each one of us. I finished praying for someone and was ready to take the next person in line when a young man, about twenty-seven or twenty-eight years old, pushed in from the side of the line. I was thinking he was a bit rude when the Holy Spirit corrected me by reminding me of the woman with the issue of blood. She was desperate, and so was this young man. He had a bump about three-fourths of an inch out the back of his jaw on the right side. He said he broke his jaw three years ago, and it hadn't healed correctly. Since then, it had been painful for him to eat. I reminded him of an earlier testimony of a jaw that had been healed and said that God would do it again. I put my hand on the bump and began to pray. It was a protruding bone that was hard and stationary. After praying a minute or so, the bump started to move, and then it softened and receded. As I continued to press in, the bone grew smaller. When I asked if he was still experiencing pain, he said that he wouldn't know until he ate something. So I said, "Let's get some food and try it." The man behind him pulled out a piece of taffy and gave it to him. He began to chew and said there was no pain, but there was a popping in the back of his jaw. By this time my wife, Linda, had joined us in prayer. When she heard the popping sound, she reached up and commanded the popping to stop in the name of Jesus, and it stopped! We then asked, "No pain and no popping?" He replied, "Yes!" Then he reached up and felt his cheek where the bump had been and became very excited, telling the translator, "It's gone! The bump is gone!"

Michael

Pastor

Youth Power Invasion trip to São Paulo, Brazil

Crohn's Disease

I (Randy Clark) was teaching at meetings in Slough, England. At one point I shared the testimony of a man who had been healed of Crohn's disease. He had visible proof verified by his doctors. As I was sharing this testimony, a woman on the front row was overcome by the presence of the Holy Spirit. She felt fire in her stomach and went down to the floor. Come to find out she wasn't the one who was sick—it was her sister that had Crohn's disease. Later, she called her mother and told her what had taken place. The mother brought the sister with Crohn's disease, who was an unbeliever, for prayer the following night. I didn't find out what happened until later, when I received a letter from the sister. Here is a paraphrase of their testimony: When you were praying you just skipped right by my sister. I wanted to yell, "Randy, come back! You need to be the one to pray for her!" But I felt the Holy Spirit say, "Don't look to the man. Look to me! Don't call Randy back." Then a young teenage girl came up and said, "Is something wrong with you?" I thought to myself, "God, if it is not going to be Randy, let it at least be a pastor or someone on the staff, not a teenage girl!" But I said nothing. The teenage girl began to pray and instantly my sister was healed!"

Do not hear me (Randy) say that there are not people more anointed than others. Do not here me say that I believe in the egalitarian view of the church, that everyone is equal in their gifts, callings, or anointing. I believe in the five-fold ministry. But I believe the five-fold ministry is to equip the saints for the work of the ministry. If we are gifted and graced with a ministry position, I believe the grace that came to us can come to the people, and we're to give it away!

Told by Randy Clark in *The Thrill of
Victory and The Agony of Defeat*

Dental Issues; Tooth Partially Grown In

Tonight after Randy released the team to pray, I decided to stand next to Randy because I could see it was a hotspot of anointing. A teenager with braces on her teeth came up to me for prayer. On her right upper jaw there was a large gap where a tooth was missing. She lifted her lip and showed me a round projection in the upper part of her gums above the gap. She said that for two years the tooth that should have grown in had partially formed and become a projection in the gum. She was facing surgery. I felt great faith because I had asked God for the opportunity for a creative miracle. As her aunt, a cousin, and two friends looked on, I began to pray, contending with God for a miracle. I felt like Jacob contending with the angel for the blessing. As I prayed, her eyes started fluttering and she said she felt heat and electricity in her upper jaw. After a few minutes, she said she could feel a tearing inside her gum where the partially formed tooth was. She had a friend get a small hand-mirror so that she could look and inspect what was happening. When we checked her mouth, the gum at the top of the projection in her jaw was turning red. After the initial heat and electricity, she said that the area had now become numb. We continued to pray. Checking again, we were excited to see that the bump had flattened at the top and the tooth appeared to be changing position. As I prayed again, crying out for a miracle, she said she saw two bands of light appear, following the shape of her upper jaw. The tooth was continuing to change orientation and was dropping. The excitement and faith level rose higher. I prayed that Jesus would correct the socket in the bone and would make proper room for her tooth to descend. After praying more, something began to move her head around. She later told us that it felt like all of her teeth were shifting back and forth. She felt vibration and heat. As we watched the tooth descend and move, the excitement attracted a woman who spoke English. She observed for a couple of minutes and then said, "I'm a dentist." I asked her to come around where she could see more easily. As we continued to pray, the power level increased and the girl's head began to move around again. Informed that the team was leaving for the hotel in five minutes, I prayed again, then asked the dentist to check. She inspected both sides of the upper jaw and informed us that the tooth, which had changed shape and orientation as it descended in the gum, was now in the proper place to grow in normally! The girl beamed and said, "Thank you so much!" in English as she gave me a couple of big bear hugs. What a celebration we had!

Dennis

Software Engineer

Global Awakening mission trip to Brazil

Dental Issues; Tooth/Jaw Pain

I prayed for three people in the hallway with a team member from Australia. The first two were women who had responded to a word of knowledge regarding tooth/jaw pain. After ten to fifteen minutes of prayer for each of them, they both left 100 percent healed.

Linda
Global Awakening mission trip to China

Dental Issues; Painful Tooth; Salvation

A man came for prayer for a toothache. I felt led to ask him if he was a Christian. He said no, he was only there because his wife had brought him. I asked if he wanted to receive Jesus as his Savior. He said, "No, maybe later." I said that Jesus puts no conditions on His healing; He loves everyone. The man received prayer, and his tooth pain went away. When I asked again if he wanted to receive Jesus as his Savior, he said, "Yes" and prayed the salvation prayer.

Kathy
Homemaker
Global Awakening mission trip to China

Digestive Disorders; Hemorrhoids

When I first preached on the theme of acts of obedience releasing power for healing, I had an odd impression that occurred while I was worshiping, just before I was to get up and preach the message. The impression was that there were people in the service suffering from digestive issues. Following this impression, I received a mental picture of people bending forward and backward, almost to the ground. I felt God was telling me to instruct those with digestive issues to do this and He would heal them. I quietly asked the Lord how long I should have the people do this. He didn't give me an answer so I felt like He was leaving that up to my judgment. My judgment was that we needed to do it long enough to feel very foolish but not so long that anyone would pass out. None of this really made sense to my logical mind. However, I really felt like we were to obey the voice of the Lord for the healings to occur. It didn't need to make sense. It was to be an act of faith.

When worship was over, I went to the platform and shared the impression. There were about a thousand people in the meeting that night. My guess was that twenty to thirty people might come up front for this particular healing, but to my surprise about two hundred people came forward for healing for digestive problems! Remembering First Corinthians 14:40 that tells us that everything should be done *"decently and in order"* (ESV), I decided it was best to spread out those in need of healing, lining them up about seven feet apart. I didn't want people bending over and bumping into those around them.

When the Lord gave me the impression and mental picture during worship, I realized that this healing was for me as well. I had been bleeding pretty badly for two months and was afraid I was developing some sort of cancer or other serious digestive issue. God's healing is always for everyone—the one teaching and giving the word and those receiving it.

So there we stood, foolishly but obediently bending back and forth for over two minutes. Many of the people who came up for healing that night were totally healed by the power of God, including me. I had no more bleeding from that point on. All types of digestive problems were healed as we obeyed the word of God. We received testimony from a woman who had hemorrhoids for fifty-three years and was completely healed that night. What seemed like foolishness was obedience to what God had spoken.

I believe that God speaks today, and just as He did in the past, He often asks us to do things that don't really make sense to our natural minds. He is looking for faith, and He will create situations that allow us to express our faith. At the wedding in Canaan, the servants had to draw the water and then the miracle came. We had to bend forward and backward for about two minutes, and then God released His healing into our bodies. Do whatever He is telling you to do today, and expect to receive your healing.

Told by Randy Clark in *Healing Out
of Intimacy/Acts of Obedience*

Gallstones

I prayed for a woman who was suffering from gallstones. She had had some of them "blasted," but they had not gotten all of them. The remaining stones and large pieces had dug into her system. When I prayed, she said she felt a finger touch the large pieces; this was followed by instant release and no further pain.

Kenton
Pastor
Global Awakening mission trip to Brazil

Irritable Bowel Syndrome

I'm writing this down a week after the fact because I had to test it out. This time the person who got healed was me. Seven years ago, I had a severe stomach virus that damaged the nerves in my intestines. It gave me extreme pain in my gut, soreness, and body aches; I couldn't keep food down. It often kept me from sleeping at night. The pain was exhausting. It took everything out of me. I couldn't handle bright light, noise, or movement after being sick—like a person with migraines. The doctors have no cure for this kind of thing. They call it IBS. The only thing you can do is to avoid stress, get plenty of sleep, and stick to a special diet. I couldn't have caffeine, orange juice, pizza, or any spicy, rich, greasy, or acidic food. If I stayed up late or was out in the heat or worried about something, it flared up. My junior year in high school I threw up every single day at school. I couldn't stop it so I just learned to live with the pain.

All my life I have wanted to travel and have had a call to missions. I've heard the call again and again over the past two years but wondered how it could be possible. After the first couple days on this Youth Power Invasion trip, I started to get sick. I was horribly sick by the tenth day and could hardly get out of bed. I missed the worship service and was in too much pain to sit during the message. Jamie was speaking that day on healing. There were angels wandering around the church touching and healing people. Anyone who felt the power of God would stand up, and Jamie would bless that person. I begged God to send an angel with healing for me. For days I had been telling God, "Either You've got the wrong person for missions, or You have to do something about my digestive issues." I felt an angel walk past twice, but while others were healed, I was not. Then, three times while Jamie was blessing someone in my section, I felt a tiny pop in my intestine. It was something different. Then someone called out that there was a woman present who was a missionary in the Middle East and anyone who thought they were called to that part of the world should come and receive an impartation from her. The thought that went through my head was that being sick in the Middle East would be a hundred times worse than here in Brazil, but I went up anyway. When this woman prayed for me, I felt something break over my head; then I felt a warm liquid running slowly down my face and ears. It was a physical sensation, but there was nothing there. It felt like oil. Then I felt a yanking and pulling in my left side where the pain had been earlier. I think it was an angel at work. Afterward the yucky sick feeling was gone. I decided to test the healing. I started eating sausage and onions for breakfast and drinking coke and coffee. I ate everything! There has been no pain at all for a week, and there's a definite change in my waistline! It used to be hard for me to gain weight. I had to eat all the time to feel satisfied. Now I can return to normal eating habits!

Elizabeth, age twenty
Global Awakening Youth Power Invasion
trip to Curitiba, Brazil

Liver Pain

A Brazilian woman came up to me last night and wanted prayer for pain in her liver. I prayed for Holy Spirit to come and bring His healing anointing. The Lord touched her, and she told me all the pain left at the name of Jesus.

Lisa
Church Janitorial Staff
Global Awakening mission trip to Brazil

Rash in Mouth; High Fever

An infant boy was brought to us for prayer. He was fussy and clinging to his mom. It's so difficult when babies are sick because they can't tell you what they need or how they feel, and this child's frustration was reflected in his eyes. He had a high fever that had caused a rash inside his mouth, making it painful for him to swallow. We prayed and commanded the sickness to be gone. As we prayed, the peace of God came upon him and he became silent and still. I asked the mother what we could do to see if he was healed, and she asked her husband to go get his bottle. Before the husband returned with the bottle, the baby grabbed my translator's water out of her hand and forced her cup up to his mouth. He drank a bunch of sips and didn't cry at all as he swallowed. He appeared to be healed!

Rose, age nineteen
Student
Global Awakening Brazil Youth Power
Invasion trip to São Paulo, Brazil

Stomach Tumors

An older man came up to me and said he had tumors on the side of his stomach that had caused him a lot of pain for over a year. I asked the Holy Spirit to come and bring more anointing for healing. Then I told the pain to leave and commanded healing in Jesus's name. I asked the man how he felt, and he motioned with his hands that he felt the tumors shrink to nothing and that he was pain-free. He was so happy he gave us a hug with tears in his eyes.

Matt
Global Awakening Mission trip to Londrina, Brazil

Throat—Dry Throat; No Saliva

It was the second evening of our trip, and my group went to hear the preaching. Afterwards people on the team gave words of knowledge, and then we went out into the crowd to start praying for people. I saw a woman standing up, and since no one was around her, I went to pray for her. I didn't have a translator at the time, but she had her hands on her throat so I figured that the problem was there. I started praying for God to heal her throat. After a few minutes, I turned around and signaled a translator to come over. The translator said that this woman had no saliva and whenever she ate or drank, her food would get stuck in the middle of her throat. I started praying, and after a few minutes I stopped and asked her how she was feeling. She said that she felt the same so I continued to pray for her. After a couple of minutes, she started talking to the translator saying that she was 100 percent healed. She was able to swallow. I led her onto the stage to give her testimony. She told the translator onstage that her doctor told her she would have to get her glands surgically removed and recovery would take two weeks. She told her doctor that she couldn't have the surgery because she couldn't afford to be without work that long. She also told the translator that before she came to the meeting, she had prayed and asked God for a miracle. Well, she got it! And now she is completely healed.

Brytne
Global Awakening mission trip to Brazil

Throat—Lumps in Throat

A young man in his mid-twenties who spoke English asked for prayer for two lumps on both sides of his throat. I prayed for him for about thirty seconds and then asked if his throat was better. He felt his throat and said in a surprised voice that the lumps had shrunk. I then prayed again and asked him to check again. He checked his throat and told me the lumps had completely disappeared. My interpreter said he should immediately go and give his testimony, but because there were so many people waiting for prayer it was not possible to escort him to the stage.

Frank
Art Dealer
Global Awakening mission trip to India

Ulcer

There was a man who asked God to give a word of knowledge in the meeting so he would know he had been healed. I gave a word of knowledge for stomach pain, and he came up and said he had an ulcer. We prayed, he felt fire, and all the pain disappeared! I also saw the ulcer fall out (prophetically).

Bethany

Student

Global Awakening mission trip to Brazil

ENDOCRINE SYSTEM

The ENDOCRINE SYSTEM consists of glands that distribute hormones by means of the circulatory system for the metabolism of all body tissues (thyroid) and the regulation of the development or activity of certain organs (pituitary). The hypothalamus regulates thirst, hunger, sleep, and emotions. The thyroid and parathyroid glands regulate metabolism, protein synthesis, growth and development, sexual function, strength and rate of heartbeat, and consumption of oxygen. The adrenal glands produce adrenaline, aldosterone, and cortisol. The pancreas converts food to body fuel, aids digestion, and regulates blood sugar. The ovaries, ovarian follicles, and corpus luteum are regulated by the endocrine system, as are the testicles, which are responsible for testosterone production.

Jesus summoned His twelve disciples and gave them authority over unclean spirits, to cast them out, and to heal every kind of disease and every kind of sickness.
—MATTHEW 10:1 NASB.

Diabetes; Lameness; Stomach Pain; Salvation

We prayed for a lady in a wheelchair who has not been able to walk for five years because her legs were affected by diabetes. She said she also had pain in her stomach area for five years. As we prayed she felt heat, and then the pain in her stomach disappeared. She also felt heat in her legs. We asked her to try and stand, which she had not done for five years. She stood and was able to walk a few steps. Her legs were very weak from lack of use, but she was so happy! We were then able to lead her in a prayer for her salvation!

Carolyn
Homemaker
Global Awakening mission trip to Mexico

Diabetes-Related Foot Infection

About eight months ago I was in Mercy Medical Hospital in Redding, California, due to an infection in my foot from diabetes. It was the second time I had been there in two days. The ER doctor came in and said that they wanted to keep me so they could watch the infection to make sure it didn't get worse because if it did, they would likely have to amputate the foot. The next day I woke up and my foot was twice as bad! In a panic, I was preparing to head back to the ER when I got a phone call from a friend. She said, "Instead of going to the ER come to the Randy Clark healing conference," so I did, and this is what happened:

I walked in on crutches just as the first testimony was being given. It was about a man getting his foot cut off, sewed back on, and being healed. I sat down, and the ushers propped my foot up to elevate it because the pain was intense. When I looked to my right, the lady sitting there was the doctor from the ER. Neither of us could believe it! I started to cry, and the doctor prayed for me. The next day when I awoke, my infection was completely gone!! I went to my regular doctor two weeks later to tell him what happened, and he told me it was completely impossible; an infection like that would take at least two to three weeks to leave the body. Then he told me that my blood work just came back, and that my A1C's are 5.5, which means that I am in the 1 percent of diabetics who beat diabetes—the diabetes was gone!!! I trusted in God, and not only did He take my infection, but He took my diabetes!!! Since that night I went from five shots of insulin a day to none!

I gave my life to Jesus that day five years ago, and since then I have witnessed too many miracles to count. God shows up every single day. I have been totally healed of every medical problem. At forty-eight years old, I am healthier now than I have ever been and am riding my longboard sometimes fifty miles a day! Praise God. God is good, and *everyone* needs to know just how good He is!

Darrin

Parkinson's Disease

I prayed for an elderly lady with Parkinson's disease who had weakness in the left side of her body that was hindering her ability to walk. God began to heal her, but her arm continued to tremble. I kept praying and waiting for God to complete her healing, but she continued to shake. Finally, it dawned on me that the tremors could be the Holy Spirit. I let go of her hand, and she stopped shaking. Praise be to God! She was able to walk out of the church, walking strongly without any tremors or weakness.

Nancy
Homemaker
Global Awakening mission trip to Brazil

Parkinson's Disease

An older woman came to me with back and neck pain. She could not raise her right arm more than just a little and could not clench her hand into a fist at all. We saw some improvement through prayer, especially in raising her arm. I thought it was arthritis or bursitis. Later I heard she'd gone to a number of team members that night, and each time there was more improvement. The next night she came up to me beaming and jabbering in Russian, grabbing my hand so tightly it hurt. A translator listened briefly and said, "She's been healed!" I then realized the hand she was clutching me with was the hand that had not closed at all the night before! She had complete freedom of movement and was so happy. I praised God with her and was walking off when someone came up to me and said, "You do not understand. That woman had Parkinson's disease. This is big miracle!"

Holly
Missionary
Global Awakening mission trip to Ukraine

Parkinson's Disease; Broken Back; Concussion; Seizures/Epilepsy

In 1979, at the age of twenty-two, I was involved in an auto accident and suffered numerous internal injuries, including a broken back and a severe brain concussion. As a result of these injuries, I have suffered physically for the last twenty-seven years. During this period of time I was hospitalized over fifty-five times and had over thirty-two surgeries. In the mid 1980s, I began having seizures, which were diagnosed as epilepsy as a result of the head trauma suffered in the accident. Years later, as the seizures subsided, I was diagnosed with Parkinson's disease. The years of illness have taken a toll on my family finances, my relationships, and my quality of life. My wife has spent countless hours in doctors' waiting rooms and surgery and ICU waiting rooms, some-times not knowing if I would live or not. Pain, slowness of movement, Parkinson's, and illness had become a way of life for me.

At a young age, I felt a call of God on my life to preach, teach, and share the Gospel. In spite of all the injuries and hospital visits, I have been involved in ministry these twenty-seven years. After serving as a pastor, youth pastor, worship leader, and evangelism director, I felt the call to go on the mission field in 1991. Answering the call, I traveled and ministered in India, Africa, and Central America. After attending revival services at Brownsville Assembly of God in Pensacola in 1994 and having a new encounter with the Holy Spirit, my wife and I served with International Gospel Outreach (IGO), a mission agency based out of Mobile, Alabama. Through IGO we ministered in Honduras, India, Tanzania, and Kenya. Later, God lead us to start our own min-istry—the Great Commission Center Medical Mission. We recovered used medical equipment and supplies from hospitals and doctors that were destined to be discarded. We also collected donations of medica-tions from pharmaceutical companies and hospitals. We would ship these supplies to Third World countries and organize and lead medi-cal mission teams of Christian doctors, nurses, and lay people who set up medical clinics in the remote bush of Tanzania, Kenya, Uganda, and Sudan. These clinics were used as evangelism and church-planting tools. Looking back, it's amazing I have been able to do the things I have done in spite of the pain and physical suffering. I have traveled and minis-tered in over twenty-six different countries. Over the years, it has been a vicious cycle of going to the mission field, returning home, going into the hospital, getting better, going back to the field, returning home, back into the hospital, and on and on.

It is by the grace of God that I have done any of these things. I have laid my hands on others and prayed for healing in Africa and seen God do great healings while questioning why He did not heal me. The whole time there was always a feeling inside me that God had much more for me. I felt as if I was being suppressed and held back from being who God intended me to be. I would go just so far, do so much, achieve certain goals, only to be knocked down by my physical sufferings and limitations. In the last three years, my ability to travel and minister has been greatly curtailed as a result of the progression of the Parkinson's disease. I was not able to travel or minister after returning from Kenya in July 2004. I felt as if I was a fish out of water, lying on the shore, unable to move. I had so much to preach, teach, and share, with no outlet to do so. In March 2005, after a five-week hospital stay with three surgeries and three weeks of being in a coma, knocking at death's door, I returned home to sit idle and recover, resolved that my life in ministry was over. Was God through with me? As the Parkinson's disease progressed, I felt useless, helpless, and worthless as I watched my wife carry the burden of being the father, mother, breadwinner, and leader of our family. Anger and bitterness rose up inside of me that affected my relationship with my wife and children and everyone around me.

Sunday, February 26, after worship, my pastor announced that he wanted to take me to Fort Worth, Texas, to attend the Amber Rose Healing Conference to receive healing from Parkinson's disease. He asked the church for prayer and help with funds for us to make the trip. I was very excited about the possibility of going to the conference to be ministered to and to hear the great speakers. Jack Taylor was one of the conference speakers. He had experienced a significant healing in his life after a visit to Toronto in 1994. Bill Johnson, pastor of Bethel Church, was another one of the speakers. He had witnessed an unprecedented number of miraculous healings and an outpouring of the Holy Spirit in Redding, California. Also on the docket was Randy Clark, who was used by God to initiate a move of the Holy Spirit in 1994 at a small storefront church near the Toronto Airport in Canada. This move of the Spirit has become a worldwide revival, impacting millions.

I was greatly encouraged that everyone at church was praying for me. I wanted so much to be healed.

After church that day, my family and I went out for dinner. Only moments after eating my meal I felt a sharp pain in my abdomen, as if someone had run a sword through my body. As each minute passed, the pain became more severe. With no relief, I was taken to the hospital, only to have emergency surgery later that afternoon. Awakening in the ICU the next morning, I felt defeated and that any chance for me to go to the conference on healing had been smothered. In the days to come, I stated to my wife that I felt washed up. I was ready to die. In fact, I was crying out to God in my suffering and pain, "God, You've got to heal me. If not, then kill me!" It was obvious this was a direct attack by the enemy in an effort to keep me from traveling to Southlake, Texas, to attend the conference. The church pressed in and continued to pray.

After coming home from the hospital, I was only able to eat very small amounts and take small sips of water and was still in considerable pain. At this point, I had lost over twenty-five pounds in three weeks and was very weak. All of this combined with my Parkinson's made it extremely hard to move. My hope of attending the Amber Rose Conference were growing dimmer. The day before we were set to leave for the conference, the pain was severe. I was in agony. I called my pastor for prayer, and my wife activated the prayer chain. Later in the day, the pain became even more intense, with some signs of intestinal bleeding. I called my doctor's office that afternoon, knowing that by placing the call I would be admitted immediately to the hospital again. The nurse placed me on hold to summon the doctor. While on hold I felt as if God was speaking to me, saying, "Trust Me! Trust Me." I immediately hung up the phone and began to pray, "God, heal me!! Allow me to go to the conference!"

Late that evening, after being restless and in severe pain all day, I finally fell asleep. While sleeping, I had a dream that there was a great crowd of people lined up on each side of a street, pressing in to try to see someone coming in a great procession. As the image came closer, I realized that everyone was trying to see Jesus. He was dressed in beautiful robes of brilliant white. It was an absolute pure bright-white color, the likes of which I have never seen before. It was brighter than the sun, yet soothing and peaceful when I looked directly at Him. Everyone wanted to touch Him, and they were crying out, "Lord! Lord!" Immediately, I remembered the woman in the Bible who suffered from the issue of blood. "If only I could touch the hem of His garment, I will be healed!" she said. I then started to push my way through the crowd. Reaching out with my right hand, I stretched out my arm as far as I could through a small hole that opened between the shoulders, arms, and heads of the people in front of me. As Jesus passed by, I felt a small brush of fabric flow across the tops of my fingers. Immediately, I found myself awake, lying on my back with my right arm reaching straight out into the air as it had been in the dream. It was almost as if it had really happened! When I sat up, I realized that the pain in my abdomen was almost gone. Then I fell back to sleep until the alarm woke me a few hours later.

The following morning, I made it to the airport, and as my pastor and I were checking in, a dear friend and intercessor from our church arrived to see us off. She asked if we could share communion together before we left. Immediately, I recalled hearing evangelist Perry Stone make a statement that the Lord's Supper is "the meal that heals." She proceeded to open a small bag and remove juice and crackers for us. There, in the middle of the airport terminal, my pastor prayed as the three of us shared communion. As I thought about the suffering body and the shed blood of Jesus Christ, I was reminded that His suffering was for me—not only for my sins, but also for my physical infirmities. I prayed that God would give me strength to make the journey ahead.

We arrived at Gateway Church, made our way inside, and found two empty seats just to the right of center on the second row. The seats in the row in front of us were empty when we arrived, only to be filled by none other than Bill Johnson, Randy Clark, and Jack Taylor. What a God-orchestrated setup! As Jack Taylor took his seat, he turned to me, reached out and took my hands, and told me that he loved me and that God loves me. Then he said, "God is going to touch you tonight. Are you ready to receive from the Lord?" Tears filled my eyes, and hope rose in me. Jack Taylor was the first speaker of the day. He began by talking about the great love of God in Christ Jesus. Then he turned, looked directly at me, and said, "I love you, and God is going to touch you tonight." Great expectancy rose inside of me, along with a strong sense of the presence of the Holy Spirit. Jack spoke about the Kingdom of God and the Model Prayer that Christ gave us to pray. During his message I began to pray, "Thy Kingdom come NOW in my life! Come into my physical body!" I cried out to God for Him to be glorified in my body! I wanted His Kingdom and everything He had for me. I just had to have it! Just as I had prayed a few days earlier, I declared, "Lord, heal me or kill me!" It was if I had grabbed hold of God and I was not going to let go of Him until He did something for me.

The next speaker was Bill Johnson. He also spoke about the Kingdom of God and His power to heal. Only a few minutes into his message, he abruptly stopped and stated: "There is someone here experiencing severe pain in their abdomen, and God wants to take that away from you right now." I said to myself, "Hey, that's me!" and immediately pushed my hand into the air. Bill asked Jack and Randy Clark to pray for me. He had the entire crowd point their hands toward me and pray. Jack Taylor placed his hands on my stomach, and Randy placed his hands on my head. Both of them spoke softly and lovingly. Jack prayed for a healing touch from God as Randy spoke against the pain and the root cause with authority, commanding it to leave. As they prayed, I felt a warmth and slight burning sensation in my abdomen. They prayed for about four minutes and then asked me how I felt. I realized that the pain was gone! As I sat there in my seat, I rejoiced and thanked the Lord for what He had done. Then I remembered the original reason we had come to the conference—for me to receive healing from Parkinson's disease. The most recent abdominal surgery and constant pain were just an attack by the enemy to keep me from receiving from God, but now it was gone and I was free to receive God's complete healing.

I resumed praying, "Thy Kingdom come NOW in my life! Thy Kingdom come NOW in my body! Increase Your Kingdom in me, Lord!" Bill resumed speaking and after a few minutes was interrupted again by the Lord. He stopped and made a statement that sometimes people are involved in accidents and receive injuries and a spirit of infirmity takes over their body that causes them to suffer for many years. My pastor, knowing my background and history, leaned over and tapped Jack on the shoulder, telling him that Bill was talking about me. Jack stood up and said, "Bill, that would be this man sitting right here," pointing to me. When Bill asked for more information regarding my condition, my pastor stood up and gave a quick medical history. With that, Randy Clark turned and proceeded to whisper into my ear, relating the testimony of a woman who was healed of advanced Parkinson's. Bill instructed the crowd to extend their hands again and pray for me. As they prayed, Jack and Randy laid hands on me and began to pray, commanding the infirmity to leave my body. Randy asked God to regenerate the cells in my brain and restore my entire neurological system. Suddenly I felt heat in my head that began to burn. Then the burning sensation moved through my head, down my neck, through my body, and down my legs. As it proceeded, it intensified into a hot fire burning inside of me. I felt as if my entire body was on fire, but at the same time it was peaceful and soothing. Again, the presence of the Holy Spirit came over me with a great heaviness. As Randy and Jack continued to pray, the burning sensation gradually subsided. My clothes were saturated with sweat. Then I realized that I was holding my head straight up. I was no longer looking at the floor! My whole body felt as light as a feather. I immediately stood up to my feet and felt a steadiness that I had not felt in years. Was this it? Did I get it? Oh my God! Yes! Yes! It happened! The whole place praised God for my healing. As Bill resumed talking, the Holy Spirit began to speak to me, telling me to get rid of my cane. Then it hit me—I had taken ownership of the Parkinson's disease, and the cane was a sign of that ownership. I got out of my seat and walked upright to the front and center of the room and proceeded to throw down the cane as hard as I could right in front of the podium. Bill pointed to me as I walked away and declared, "It is finished! It is over! It is done!"

The next day at the conference, I was able to walk upright unassisted with no tremors. As I sat in my seat, I was overwhelmed with sadness by memories of what my wife and family had endured over the years as a result of my illness. Then that same feeling I had experienced the day before when I was healed came over me. It was then that God, in His great love, wrapped His arms around me and spoke to my heart as a loving father would. He said, "Lee, I am going to rewrite your history. Everything that the enemy has stolen from you over the past twenty-seven years I'm going to return to you sevenfold! Any ground he has taken in your relationships with your wife and your children will be restored! You will be restored financially, emotionally, spiritually, and physically! It will be as if none of these things has ever happened!"

Returning home after the conference, I found my strength increasing daily. When I shared my testimony at church, word of God's miracle healing began to spread throughout our town. At one point during the service, I felt the urge to run. Jumping from my seat I began to run up and down the aisles. Seeing this, my nine-year-old daughter began to cry, for she had never seen her dad run before. She cried tears of joy for almost three hours. I am now running around like a sixteen-year-old kid. Before leaving the conference in Dallas, Randy laid hands on me and prayed for an impartation. God has opened up so many doors for ministry as a result of my healing. The doctors who were treating me were so amazed and astonished that they are now giving testimony of what happened to me to many of their patients. I am going to the local hospitals weekly to pray for people, and we are seeing people healed. Often doctors call me to come pray for their patients, or the families call me. We now have plans to open a healing room at our church. I am leading several of our members through the Global Awakening Ministry training manuals. Praying for the sick has become commonplace in our church and on the streets of our city. We are seeing God do wonderful and amazing things. I thought I was all washed up in ministry and that God was through with me, but now I am preaching and teaching about the Kingdom of God and His healing power in different churches almost every week. Doors have opened up for me to speak at denominational churches—from Baptist and Pentecostal to Catholic churches. The head of a local Catholic hospital is having me speak to all the physicians on staff at a luncheon on healing. I have seen many come to a personal relationship with Jesus and many healed of everything from arthritis to tumors. God is so good. Pray that I always point to Him as the Source and the Healer.

Lee

Lee's full testimony can be found at www.thehealedguy.com

Parkinson's Disease

This particular healing took place while I was in the middle of a forty-day fast specifically for creative miracles. As I share this testimony, I need to say that I didn't initially feel any compassion for this woman about whom I am about to tell you. In fact, I was kind of angry with her to begin with. I was preaching a message on impartation titled "Spend and Be Spent." At one point I asked those in need of healing to go up to the balcony to be prayed for by our ministry team. I wanted to reserve the front of the church for those who were feeling a call to the mission field, specifically those under twenty-nine years of age. That was when Anne came up to me for prayer. She wasn't twenty-nine. She was forty-nine, but she looked as if she was sixty-nine. She was shaking terribly and asked me to pray for her. "I'm not going to pray for healing tonight," I said. "If you need healing, go to the balcony and someone will pray for you there."

"I've already been to the balcony, and someone prayed for me and I didn't get healed," she replied. "God told me if I came to the meeting tonight and you prayed for me, He would heal me. I am in the last stages of Parkinson's disease, and if I don't get healed, I don't want to live any longer," she said. With that, I began to pray, asking the Holy Spirit to come. Anne fell to the floor and lay there without shaking. I asked her husband if it was normal for her to stop shaking, and he explained that the only time she stopped shaking was when she was in a deep sleep. I thought resting in the Spirit would be equal to a deep sleep, and so I went to pray for others but was constantly drawn back in my mind to Anne. Each time I went back to where she lay on the floor I would kneel down, lay hands on her, and bless her.

Then it hit me—here was someone in need of a creative miracle, and I was in the middle of a forty-day fast specifically for creative miracles! I knelt down and put my hand on her head and said, "O God, I call those things that are not as though they are. I need millions of new brain cells." As I prayed, she began to scream and say, "Ahhh, my head is killing me. Stop praying! My head is killing me!"

"O God," I cried, "don't listen to her prayer; listen to mine! More! More! More!" With that, Anne went completely still. "Anne, what happened?" I asked. "I don't hear anything or feel anything," she replied in a very quiet voice. "All I know is that you're here, Jesus is here, and Elvis (her husband) is here." Then she began to test herself for symptoms of Parkinson's. She got up and drank water from a cup, which was significant because previously she could only sip through a straw. Then she asked if she could go up onstage. I thought that because God had just healed her, she could do anything she wanted—she was queen for a day! Up onstage Anne began to stomp her foot and say, "Look at this, I couldn't do this before." Taking her husband's hand, she said, "Look at this. I can squeeze my husband's hand." She then talked about going home and holding her two-year-old grandson whom she had never held before for fear of dropping him. Then she surprised us all by playing the piano. She was quite good. She went on to tell us that before her illness, she used to play the piano and Elvis would sing. One day she stopped playing in the middle of his singing because she couldn't remember anything. She was so embarrassed that she ran offstage. A visit to the doctor revealed she had Parkinson's disease. She hadn't played the piano from that point on until the night she was healed. Sitting there at the keyboard that night in front of everyone, she began to sing: "He touched me, and oh, the joy that floods my soul. For something happened, and I know He's touched me and made me whole." Though she couldn't sing very well, there was not a dry eye in the whole place.

Told by Randy Clark in his sermon "The Thrill of Victory"

IMMUNE SYSTEM

The peripheral IMMUNE SYSTEM includes the lymph nodes, spleen, and the neuroimmune system, which is composed of cells within the brain that mediate interactions between systems of the body in reaction to invasive and harmful pathogens.

But You, O Lord, are a shield about me,
my glory, and the lifter of my head.
—PSALM 3:3 ESV

Arthritis in Hands; Forgiveness

A woman with arthritis, high blood pressure, and high cholesterol came for prayer. The arthritis had crippled her hands so that she could not close them completely, and she had much pain in them. I felt led to begin with the crippled hands and the pain there. I spoke to the pain and the arthritis. She said she felt better almost immediately and could close her hand better than before. Remembering that arthritis and unforgiveness are often linked, I asked about any unforgiveness, and she confessed to that. We continued to pray for healing, and complete healing followed. She has no pain and can completely close her hand.

George

Pastor

Global Awakening mission trip to Brazil

AIDS; Progressive Multifocal Leukoencephalopathy

My name is Michael. My medical reports will show that I have hemophilia, asthma, and epilepsy. On April 8, 1990, I was diagnosed with full-blown AIDS and given three to five years to live. In November 1999, my condition took a sudden turn for the worse. I started having double vision so I went to my doctor, who referred me to an eye specialist. Two weeks later, I began to experience speech problems so my doctor ordered a MRI. When the results came back, I was diagnosed with progressive multifocal leukoencephalopathy (PML). Essentially, it was a death sentence. According to my doctor, he has never seen anyone who had this condition live more than a year. Only 1 percent of people with PML live more than a year, but in the end they all die from the disease.

By the end of December 1999, my condition was so bad that I was bound to a wheelchair and given morphine patches to help with the awful pain I was feeling. When my condition worsened, my doctor ordered another MRI. The new results showed that the dead tissue in my brain had doubled in size. In January 2000, my doctor had my wife and I come to his office to tell us that at the rate the PML was growing, I had six to eight weeks left to live. I was told that there was nothing else he could do for me medically except to insert a feeding tube. He took me off all my medication for AIDS. We discussed my dying wishes, including my DNR (Do Not Resuscitate) Order and my Notice of Expiration.

When my wife and I got home, I called my sister and asked her to prepare my will. I had lost hope and decided to give up fighting death any longer. My wife, however, was not ready to give up! She stood in the gap for me, believing that God would heal me. When she heard that Randy Clark was coming to our church, Suncoast Worship Center in Englewood, Florida, she took me there despite my weak condition.

I will never forget that day, January 27, 2000, when Randy Clark prayed for me. He told me about Jesus bringing Lazarus back to life. Randy said that if Jesus could heal Lazarus's dead brain, then it would be easy for Him to heal my dying brain! As Randy was praying, my six kids and my wife and I all began to weep. This was on a Friday night. Less than three days later, on Monday morning when I woke up, I noticed that all of my symptoms were gone! My sight had improved dramatically, my speech was no longer slurred, and I was able to get out of my wheelchair! My doctor was absolutely amazed. He wrote in my medical report that my recovery was nothing short of "miraculous"! My weight has gone from one hundred sixty-five pounds to two hundred and one pounds, my T cells from seventeen to three hundred sixty-five, and my viral load went from one hundred sixty thousand to eighty. And best of all, I now have eight healthy kids, the newest only three months old. Thank You, God! Since my miracle healing, I have a burden to share the love of God with as many people as I can. I am looking forward to going on a mission trip with Randy. I sent my kids on a youth mission trip last year, and they loved it! I pray that God will continue to use my healing testimony to inspire and encourage others. What an awesome God we serve!

Michael

Englewood, Florida

AIDS

God never ceases to amaze me! He is at work in so many awesome ways! Recently, I was ministering at a meeting in Ellicott City, Maryland. The Spirit of Prophecy was moving powerfully around the room and ministering all sorts of good things. Jesus was healing people and changing lives. The atmosphere was rife for miracles. At one point during the service, the Holy Spirit prompted me to call a woman out of the crowd, showing me that she had a blood disorder. Her name was Doris. I asked her if there was something wrong with her blood. She quickly ran forward and said, "Yes, I have AIDS!" I thought, "Well, that sounds like a pretty serious blood disorder to me." I was about to pray for her and sensed the gift of faith rising up within me. In front of everyone, I declared that God was healing her of AIDS, standing on Second Corinthians 4:13: *"And since we have the same spirit of faith, according to what is written, 'I believed and therefore I spoke,' we also believe and therefore speak"* (NKJV). I declared, "Jesus is healing you right now! Be healed in Jesus's name!"

As I spoke these words over her, she felt something step out of her back. A week after we prayed, she went to her doctor to have her regular blood work done. She returned for another appointment a few weeks later. To the astonishment of Doris and her doctors, the AIDS that had been ravaging her body was no longer detectable. They tried to find convenient reasons for this medical breakthrough. Some attributed it to the new medication she was taking. Of course, Doris knew beyond a shadow of doubt that it was her Jesus who healed her. The doctors told her that the AIDS virus was now undetectable and that her CD4 count had nearly doubled. CD4 counts tell the number of white blood cells within an individual's body. A healthy person has over one thousand CD4 cells. White blood cells are what AIDS attacks and destroys. In the early part of September, Doris's white blood cell count was somewhere between three hundred to four hundred. After we prayed, her CD4 count shot up to seven hundred fourteen! The doctors were simply unable to explain this miracle and told her that they have never seen anything like this before.

I decided to write about this healing testimony because it demonstrates the goodness of our Father's love toward us. He is at work, wanting our attention and focus. He wants us to realize His ways are higher than the limitations of modern medical science. He wants us to start thinking like He thinks, acting like He acts, and doing what He is doing. All of this is simply because we are His sons and daughters. He gives us access as His children to look beyond the veil and see what He is up to. What a wonderful God we serve! His ways are high above everything else. To those who are reading this right now, may the Spirit of the Lord begin to minister God's healing and miracle presence to you right now. I ask that the Spirit of grace and power would impart to you miracle anointing for your life and those around you, in the name of Jesus! In His love.

Jamie Galloway

Allergies; Forgiveness

A young lady in her twenties came for prayer. She had suffered from severe allergies and sinus infections in the past nine months since her parents had been fighting and threatening to divorce. As she forgave them, she released her fear and her anger to the Lord, asking forgiveness.

Her sinuses instantly cleared up, and she felt the peace of God like a brisk breeze in her face.

Steve

Global Awakening mission trip to Mexico

Asthma

Many years ago, when my wife and I were pioneering a church, we did something we shouldn't have done: we left our nine-year-old son, Josh, at home alone. We were too poor to afford a babysitter, didn't have any family nearby, and didn't know anyone well enough to ask them to watch our son. None of those are good excuses, but that is what we did. He was actually babysitting his four-year-old sister too! I still feel guilty about this. Nevertheless, at the time I reasoned that we were only a few miles away, and we had given our son a beeper, as this was before cell phones. I told him to beep me if anything went wrong and we would be home in a matter of minutes.

We were in the middle of a meeting at the church when Josh beeped me. I could hear him gasping on the phone, saying he couldn't breathe. He was having an asthma attack. DeAnne and I hastily explained to the folks at the church what was going on, then jumped in the car and raced home. When we got to the house, we got a call from a woman at the church named Brenda. Brenda was new to the church and just recently saved. She was not familiar with how the Spirit works or with words of knowledge. As DeAnne was on the phone talking to Brenda, I was putting Josh in a chair and praying for him. He was so sick and really having trouble breathing.

This dear woman was on the phone telling DeAnne that when we left, they began praying for us, and she got a vision that she thought might be from the Lord. In the vision, God showed her what we were supposed to do. We were to take two pieces of bread, toast them, and then put them on Josh's chest and cover them with a towel. DeAnne relayed all this to me and then said, "What do you think?" I told her I thought it had to be God because it didn't make any sense. When you think about what we find in the Scriptures—talking to a rock, putting mud in a man's eyes—then putting two pieces of toast on our son's chest in the middle of an asthma attack doesn't seem quite so crazy. None of it makes sense in the natural, but our God is the God of the supernatural.

Then DeAnne asked me something that illustrates an important principle. She asked me if we should butter the toast. Now, many of you may be smiling at this, but her question is very important because it illustrates a principle that we need to understand if we are to press into the miraculous. We are to do *exactly* what Jesus tells us to do. Brenda did not see us buttering the toast in the vision. She made no mention to DeAnne of buttering the toast, and so we were not supposed to do it.

Even though the Lord's instructions to Brenda made no sense, we made the decision to follow them exactly. We made the toast and put it on Josh's chest. He was wheezing very hard at that point. Then we took a big towel and put it on top of the toast. As soon as the towel touched his chest he reared up and threw up. I caught everything neatly in the big towel, and Josh was fine after that. It was then that I remembered that the doctors had told us that when someone is in the middle of a severe asthma attack, if you can get them to throw up, their system will release the chemicals necessary to dilate their bronchial tubes. It worked! As crazy as it sounded in the natural, when we followed God's instruction exactly, the miraculous happened.

Told by Randy Clark in *Healing Out of Intimacy/Acts of Obedience*

Polio

During ministry time, a man with polio came to me for prayer. He was unable to move his right arm. We prayed for him, and his fingers began to move. This was a good sign, and it built faith. We prayed again that

God would increase the healing, then asked him to move his arm, and he was able to move it! Praise the Lord!

Jill
Real Estate Agent
Global Awakening mission trip to India

Rheumatic Fever; Joint Pain

I was with a Global Awakening team in Brazil when God gave me my first word of knowledge. I received it as a physical sensation of pain in the middle two fingers of my left hand, and it was moving up to my elbow. Randy Clark called team members to the front to give words of knowledge, and then he called for mass healing to all who were standing in response to the words of knowledge given. A woman in the crowd made a beeline for me, and I began praying for her healing. She had suffered from pain in her joints for twelve years since a bout of rheumatic fever. The pain was most consistently felt in her middle two fingers and left elbow. Randy asked everyone to test for their healing, but this woman was still in pain. I knew that God was going to use me to bring her healing because of the word of knowledge, and so I prayed more— and she was completely healed! God built faith in both our hearts through His word of knowledge.

Eric
Pilot
Global Awakening mission trip to Brazil

Rheumatoid Arthritis

I prayed for a woman with rheumatoid arthritis, from which she had suffered since she was in her twenties. She had tried all kinds of treatment, but nothing worked. She had come to Santarém, Brazil, from Manaus, where she had undergone six months of treatment. The pain continued. She couldn't bend most of her fingers. We prayed, and God healed her. She was opening and closing her fingers and was free of pain for the first time in years—and praising God at the top of her lungs!

Terry
Global Awakening mission trip to Brazil

Sjögren's Syndrome[3]

I was at Bill Johnson's church, Bethel Church, teaching on words of knowledge. Following the teaching, I invited those who had received words to come up front and share those words. When I came to the third or fourth person in line, she said, "Water bottle." That was it— there was no explanation, just the words "water bottle." "Does that make sense to anyone?" I asked, all the while thinking, "Lord, what do we do with that word?" There happened to be a woman there with a very rare disease. Her saliva glands and tear ducts didn't work so she had to carry a water bottle with her everywhere she went. When I asked if the words "water bottle" made sense to anyone, she jumped up and said, "That's me! That word is mine!" She was healed right then and there without anyone praying for her.

Told by Randy Clark in his sermon
titled "Words of Knowledge"

Shingles

A team member asked me to join her in praying for a man who indicated that he needed physical healing. With our limited knowledge of Spanish, we could not tell exactly what the problem was. He proceeded to unbutton his shirt and showed us a rash that went from about the middle of his chest over to his side and continued around to his back. He buttoned up and at our direction laid his hand on the area, and we laid hands on his hand and started praying. His hand soon started to

---

3 Sjögren's syndrome is an autoimmune disease that attacks the glands that make saliva and tears.

shake in the area of the rash. Actually, his whole chest area on that left side was shaking, and the shaking became more violent as we prayed for more of the Holy Spirit. At one point, he seemed to have to exert a good deal of energy to keep his hand from falling off his chest. We kept praying, "More Lord, more" and rebuking the pain until all of it was gone. He and his wife were overjoyed. We were very happy too! Also, I was very curious to know what condition he had been healed of, but alas, our language skills weren't good enough to understand. The next day, I saw the wife again at the church, and we found someone to interpret for us. It turns out that her husband had been healed of shingles, which is an extremely painful condition. He had been in severe pain for two months. His wife excitedly confirmed that all the pain had left the night before and had not returned. He was totally healed and feeling completely better. Thank You, Lord!!

Wendy

Lawyer

Global Awakening mission trip to Cuba

INTEGUMENTARY SYSTEM

The INTEGUMENTARY SYSTEM consists of the skin, exocrine glands, nails, and hair.

And the very hairs on your head are all numbered.
So don't be afraid; you are more valuable to
God than a whole flock of sparrows.
—LUKE 12:7 NLT

Cysts on Wrist and Hand; Lump on Hand; Pain in Joints

I prayed for a woman who had cysts on her hand and wrists. She was just standing there with her eyes open, and I was thinking, "God, I don't think she thinks You can heal her, so come and fill her with Your presence." I went on praying for her, and it was a short prayer. Then I felt something move in her wrists and hands so I closed the prayer and had the translator ask how the cysts were. She said they were gone and there was no more pain. She immediately got happy and her attitude changed. She couldn't believe it. Later she took me to one of her friends, who had a lump on his hand. I prayed, and it got 50 percent better, but it was not completely healed. I prayed for another woman later that night who had pain in her hands, knees, and elbows. I prayed for her and she felt heat so I continued praying, and she received her healing with joy.

Tasia
Global Awakening mission trip to Brazil

Eczema

A young woman came to receive prayer from eczema that was terribly irritating. It had been all over her thighs for six years. Along with another team member, I began to pray for her healing. After a couple of minutes, we stopped to ask if she felt heat or anything, and she replied, "Yes! Yes! My legs are on fire! They are burning!" We prayed, "Mais fogo," which is Portuguese for "more fire!" The Spirit fell on her, and she began to tremble and shake. We spent a few more minutes in prayer and then asked her about her condition. She said that her skin had been itching all over, but when we prayed, the itching stopped instantly! I felt like the Lord had healed her legs so that she could dance for Him pain-free and that there was a real anointing on her for that. When I shared that, she totally confirmed it and got really excited. It was great! Glory to God!!

Thomas, age seventeen
Student
Global Awakening Youth Power Invasion trip to Brazil

Ingrown Nails; Brain Cancer

During one of the ministry sessions, a word of knowledge was given for a sore big toe. A woman, about forty-five years old, came to the front with no shoes or socks and bandages on each of her big toes. The team member who had given that word of knowledge began to pray for her, and I assisted. As he prayed, he started coming against cancer. Finally, I asked if we could pray for her toes, and so he did. The woman was all smiles. The pain in her toes was gone. One nail had been removed, and another was ingrown in two places. Then she told us that she had brain cancer and God had given her a picture in her mind that as she went to receive the healing for her toes, the cancer would be defeated. The young man said that as he started to pray, the thought to pray against cancer "just appeared" and so he prayed against the cancer! This woman received a "twofer" from God—her toes were healed, and we believe she was healed of cancer too!

Bill
Global Awakening mission trip to Brazil

Skin Blotches; Self-Hate

A young woman came for prayer for blotches on her chest and legs, which we couldn't see, as they were under her clothing. As we prayed, I got the sense that she didn't like herself. She confirmed that it was true and started to weep. We ministered the Father's love to her, and she repented of disliking herself, because God loves her. We cast out a spirit of self-hatred and asked the Holy Spirit to fill her with God's love. She felt love and peace as joy swept over her. We didn't find out if the skin blotches were healed because she would have had to remove her clothes to find out.

Stacy
Missionary
Global Awakening mission trip to Ukraine

MARRIAGE AND FAMILY

The Lord God fashioned into a woman the rib which He had taken from the man, and brought her to the man. The man said, "This is now bone of my bones, and flesh of my flesh; she shall be called woman, because she was taken out of man." For this reason a man shall leave his father and his mother, and be joined to his wife; and they shall become one flesh. And the man and his wife were both naked and were not ashamed.
—GENESIS 2:22-25 NASB

Marital Problems

I was the woman on the floor up front during both services. I could not get up. My husband and I have a ministry in Rwanda. We have been at it six years, and it feels like no fruit has come forth. We've had to close the Bible college and then the preschool due to corruption, betrayal, etc. I was in the dark night of the soul. Our marriage had become strained and lifeless. The whole journey of homeschooling has been our four girls and me with my husband, who was on the outside looking in. To make matters worse, I had just been asked to be a keynote speaker at a fundraising banquet for a ministry in Nigeria to receive an award for my contributions to Africa. It seemed utterly ridiculous that they chose me, and I told them they had the wrong person. They said they still wanted me. Life at church was very grievous lately, very painful and lacking the presence of God. Every prophetic person, every intercessor, seemed to either be leaving or begging the rest of the people to stand in faith for a miracle. All I could think of was, "Why bother if the leadership does not want the presence of God?" That was my mind-set on the floor that morning. I was depressed and discouraged.

Then Randy started sharing testimonies about perseverance, and I began to feel encouraged to persevere. He talked about rowing in the boat during the night, during the storm, and getting blisters and wondering just where Jesus was. I knew that feeling. That very picture of being part of a team rowing the boat was something I had been struggling with. I always felt bad for being the one going against the "team." Randy's words gave me the strength to want to continue rowing in submission and with hope-filled faith that we are going to arrive in the presence of God!! I knew he was telling the truth when he testified that all of these trials are going to make me—make us—stronger.

After sharing these testimonies, Randy went on to tell the secrets of how a church can create an atmosphere for revival. Every single secret he shared has been the cry of my heart at our church—worship until we sense the anointing, value and equip the children, share testimonies, etc., etc., etc.!! Randy then used the Scripture about picking up your cross and bearing it to illustrate these principles. I was deeply convicted. Then I "saw" myself as the woman caught in adultery because I had been unfaithful to Christ in my responses to every one of these areas of trial. "I am so sorry," I whispered to God. "I have responded in a faithless way." On and on I prayed. As the Holy Spirit convicted my heart, I would apologize and God would forgive. It was so wonderful and powerful. Then I prayed to have my best friend back—my husband! With that, he (my husband) came and put his hand on my back as I lay face down on the floor. I knew it was him. He prayed for me and cried with me for the next two hours as God gave us a personal marriage counseling session by the Holy Spirit on the floor. We got up from that place completely different from the people that we were when we walked in. Our love was renewed! Our hope was restored! And I know that I know that I know that the best is yet to come.

Lisa and Jack
Washington Crossing Healing School

Marital Problems

This mission trip was truly a faith builder for me. I am the pastor of a relatively small mainline denominational church. Occasionally I see a few souls saved, and periodically I see a healing. I came on this trip in need of and prepared to experience the power of the Holy Spirit at work, and did I ever! Friday morning worship was the kick-off for me. It was the beginning of operating in the Spirit at a level I had never before consistently experienced. As we worshiped among the poor and outcast, the worship was both intense and sincere. Later in the day, we went to another church. The hunger for God and the expectation that He would manifest His presence was simply overwhelming.

Following the message people began to come forward and just kept coming and coming. Some sought the baptism of the Holy Spirit; others wanted more of whatever the Lord wanted to give them. Still others simply wanted to abandon themselves to Him. As I lay hands on them, they would almost immediately fall down under the influence of the Spirit. Never had ministry been so easy and so fun!

One prayer request came from a couple who were at odds with each other over various job and housing issues. After listening to both, I found myself praying that there would be unity in their decision-making and in their vision of their future. I asked the Lord to safeguard the husband's mind and then asked the wife if she would place her trust in his "bridegroom covering." At that moment, the husband went down under the anointing of the Holy Spirit. The wife then went down too. Later, they both got up, somewhat dazed and groggy. Someone in leadership told me later that he had spoken to them shortly after they had experienced the power of the Holy Spirit and they had expressed their joy at having attended the meetings with tears in their eyes and peace in their hearts.

Dave
Pastor
Global Awakening mission trip to the Middle East

MUSCULAR SYSTEM

The MUSCULAR SYSTEM consists of the muscle tissue and muscles of the body that move the head and neck; provide facial expressions; move the vertebral column; act upon the trunk; move the diaphragm; close the pelvic outlet; position and move the shoulders, arms, hands, fingers, hips, knees, ankles, and feet; control posture; and coordinate locomotion.

I will put flesh and muscles on you and cover you with skin. I will put breath into you, and you will come to life. Then you will know that I am the Lord.
—EZEKIEL 37:6 NLT

Ankle—Sprained

I sprained my ankle on the bus four days ago, and I could barely walk on it. Today I was walking along thinking, "What if God healed me right when I get to my room?" I put the key in the lock, opened the door, grabbed a snack, and sat down on my bed. Then a voice in my head said, "Take off your shoe and the ACE bandage, and you will be healed." So I did. I was not really sure what would happen so I started to walk and the pain was gone. I could even jump! I was so in shock that I called my friend to tell her what happened. I can now jump, run, leap, and do other things! Thank You, Lord!

Candice
Global Awakening mission trip to Brazil

Arm—Weak Muscles

A little boy named Gabriel, who was about five years old, was brought to me for prayer by his mother. His arms hung limp by his sides. His mother reached down and lifted his arms. His hands hung limp at the wrists, with no strength in them. I felt his hands and found no muscular response. His mother put his arms down, and they were again limp at his sides as she reached down to his leg and said something. She then turned and looked at me with a look that seemed to say, "Please help my little boy." I had no translator at the time so no history of his problem was received. Kneeling down face to face with the child, I placed one hand on each shoulder and cried out to God to heal this boy in the name of Jesus. After anointing him with oil for healing in Jesus's name, I commanded his arms, wrists, and hands to be strengthened in the name of Jesus. The Holy Spirit moved in me to speak strength into his muscles and tissues. Taking his right hand in mine, I indicated for him to move his fingers. Slowly he began to move his fingers. Strength began to return as I repeated, "In the name of Jesus, be made strong." Soon his wrists were strengthened and he was able to raise his hands with strength in his wrists. Little Gabriel and I clapped hands together, and he clapped strongly. Jesus had strengthened him and given him the use of his arms and hands. His mother stood by with tears in her eyes and a great smile of joy. We all praised God together. She motioned to his leg, indicating that one was shorter than the other. I prayed briefly and then commanded the short leg to grow out in the name of Jesus. The short leg slowly grew out until both feet were matching in length. Praise God!

Daniel

Global Awakening mission trip to Brazil

Arm—Sharp Pain

I had never received a word of knowledge before, and suddenly I had a sharp stabbing pain in my left arm. When I gave the word of knowledge, a lady responded that she had the same pain. I prayed and commanded the pain to leave, and it got worse! I continued to thank Jesus for healing, and after a few minutes she said the pain was gone! She told me that she had been praying specifically that her healing would occur during the crusade.

Caroline

Homemaker

Global Awakening mission trip to Brazil

Arm—Length Discrepancy

Okay, let's just say God is amazing! For my whole life, my right side has been longer than the left side of my body. I was showing one of my friends the difference between the length of my arms, and he suggested we pray for my shorter arm to grow. I agreed, he prayed, and nothing happened. He asked Bill Johnson to pray for me, and when Bill started to pray for my left arm, the muscles in my left arm began to fill in like they were being stretched forward to align with my right hand. As I watched this, joy came over me. It felt like a burden was lifted off of me. Praise God for touching me!

Kristi, age fifteen
Student
Global Awakening Youth Power Invasion trip to Brazil

Back—Creative Miracle

I saw a small cluster of guys pointing to their friend, who tentatively raised his hand. I went to check things out and saw a man with part of his back missing on the left side. I couldn't tell if it was actually missing or deformed. On the left side just about at his waistline there was this big indentation, which was so pronounced that I could put my hand partway into it. We were meeting in a soccer field at night, and there was very little light. I could barely see his back, only feel it. He was small, perhaps one hundred twenty pounds, but the muscles in his back were as hard as a rock, as if he might be a laborer. I called someone else on the team to come over. We prayed for a healing and a creative miracle, as we weren't sure which we needed. Very soon, his back began "moving," but not as if he was flexing his muscles. Although the man showed virtually no emotional reaction, which is very common among the Makua people, all three of us who were praying were sure that his back was "filling in." The place where the indentation had been felt much more normal. We knew we had just witnessed a wondrous miracle, and we were pretty excited.

Dale
Pastor
Global Awakening mission trip to Mozambique

Back Pain; Salvation

We were at a shopping mall one day looking for people God might want us to pray for when I saw an elderly lady sitting on a bench with her son.

I asked her if she would like us to pray for anything and if she had any pain in her body. We explained that we believed Jesus can heal and we would like to pray for her. She said she had pain in her lower back so we asked if we could put our hands on her back, and she agreed. We prayed, and her back was a little better. She told us she felt heat in that area. We told her the Lord was working in her body. We prayed again, and all the pain left her! She looked so surprised and happy. We explained that by asking Jesus into her heart, she would be right with God. He would forgive her sins, and she would know for sure that she would go to Heaven. We asked if she would like to receive Jesus, and she said, "Yes!" Her son was watching everything and paying very close attention when his mom got healed. When we asked if he would like prayer for anything, he said, "No." Then we asked if he would like to say the prayer of salvation, and he said, "Okay." So we lead him in the prayer of salvation! Yeah, God! Healing and two more souls in Heaven!

Jessica
Pastoral Assistant
Global Awakening mission trip to Brazil

Back Pain

A woman came for prayer for back pain. When I laid hands on her and prayed for her, initially she only was 50 percent better, so I pressed in, blessing what God had done and asking for 100 percent healing. Within ten minutes, she said all of the pain was gone. I hadn't felt anything during the prayer and wasn't sure she really had been healed completely because I had no translator. She went forward to share with the church what had happened. I came to find out that not only was she healed, but she could actually feel the muscles strengthening and growing stronger and correcting as she received prayer. Sometimes we aren't even aware of how powerful God's touch is through us—it's all about Him!

Heidi
Global Awakening mission trip to Brazil

Back Pain; Deafness

A grey-haired man in his seventies came for prayer for back pain and deafness in his right ear. I felt led to pray for the back pain first. The Holy Spirit was touching people all around us, and lots of people were falling down under the weight of the presence of God. My right hand began to shake. He grabbed my hand and held on to it for dear life, and he too began to shake all over. I placed my left hand over his right ear, and he stopped shaking and stood still as if paralyzed. Finally, I asked him what had happened. He said it felt like a bolt of lightning had struck him. We covered his left ear and asked if he could hear with his right ear. "I can hear, and my back pain is gone!" he shouted. He lifted his hands, praising God. Hallelujah! Glory! Praise God!

Bob
Global Awakening mission trip to Brazil

Back Pain; Forgiveness

A woman in her fifties had suffered from pain in her spine for the last three years. A word of knowledge revealed that she had anger toward God. She told us she was angry with God for a job she had lost and also over the suicide of her son. She repented of her anger and recommitted her life to the Lord. When we were done praying, the pain in her back was gone! Hallelujah!

Nancy
Counselor
Global Awakening mission trip to Argentina

Back and Shoulder Pain; Lumps in Arm; Forgiveness

A lady came forward for prayer for pain in her back and shoulders. I found out that she had been involved in several auto accidents. They were not her fault so I asked if she had ever forgiven those who had caused the accidents, and she said she had not. I led her in prayers of forgiveness, and then I prayed for healing in her back and shoulders and release from all stress and pain. When I inquired, she said all the pain was gone. Then she mentioned some lumps on her arms, which she said were caused from tightened muscles. When she felt her right arm, the lumps were gone. There was still a lump on her left arm so I prayed several times until it was almost gone. She was quite happy. I prayed again for God to complete the healing that had begun.

Laurie
Global Awakening mission trip to New Zealand

Back Pain; Emotional Wound

A man came to me for prayer for severe pains in the lower part of his back. As we were praying, God gave me a word for him. The word was about something completely different from the pain in his back—it was about something that happened in his life several years before. As we prayed together, the man started to cry and was deeply touched by the Holy Spirit. When I asked him to describe the pain in his back for me, he suddenly looked at me in surprise and said that the pain had completely disappeared; he was pain-free!

Trina
Global Awakening mission trip to Brazil

Back Pain; Herniated Disks; Metal in Spine; Broken Wrist

I am a single woman, and I live in Florida. I had been out of work and on disability due to severe back problems. I had three herniated disks and underwent a spinal fusion last year that put lots of metal in my back but did nothing to help the pain. I was on three narcotic painkillers for two and a half years, but my resistance to them made it very hard to kill the pain. My pain-control doctor warned me that whenever I did get better and needed to get off the narcotics, I would have to be admitted to the hospital for a week and be medically detoxed, otherwise I could die from the effects of sudden withdrawal on my body. I underwent every imaginable test, treatment, and procedure that you can think of to end this pain. I prayed for healing, went to numerous pastors, healing ministers, healing rooms, etc., looking for help. Nothing changed, but I had 100 percent faith in God that I had already been healed and that it would manifest itself in God's time. There was not one doubt in my mind.

In November, I went to hear Randy Clark at a healing conference in Fort Lauderdale, Florida. I went to the last night of the conference only because I had been in too much pain to attend the other nights as I had planned to do. During the forty-five minutes that I had to wait to get to Randy for prayer, the Holy Spirit did amazing things to my body. The fusion in my spine (with four titanium bolts and two titanium rods in the last two vertebrae in my back) made it difficult for me to bend over very far. As I waited for Randy, I started experiencing the crunches. They lasted for the entire forty-five minutes that I waited. I was bending so far over that my head was almost touching the ground. With the metal rods in my lower back, that was truly an amazing feat. Then I started to bend backward, which I had been unable to do after the surgery and up until this time. To make a long story short, I walked out of the church that night completely healed by the love, grace, and power of my Lord Jesus, believing that if Jesus could heal my back, He also could handle the detox. I never took another narcotic painkiller after I left the church that night, and I suffered not one single detox symptom, which is truly another miracle.

To show you how desperate the enemy is to keep us down, four days later I tripped while walking my dog and fell in the middle of the street, breaking my wrist and arm. I was admitted into the hospital for seven days and had to have surgery to put a steel rod into my arm to replace the part of the bone that had been smashed to pieces in the fall. I was also scheduled to have surgery on the wrist, which had shown up as clearly broken in the X-rays. I signed the consent forms for the wrist surgery, but when they X-rayed my wrist in the operating room, there was no break to be found. They were very confused, but I wasn't. I knew that once again I had been healed by my loving, faithful Lord Jesus.

While I was at home healing from the broken arm, I developed severe pain in my sacroiliac joint. I had experienced this once before about fifteen years ago. The doctor said there was not much he could do. On a fluke (sure it was), I happened to be up in Central Florida right before Christmas visiting my daughter. While there, I read in the local paper that in January Randy Clark was going to be doing another healing conference less than twenty miles from where I was staying. I was so excited to have the opportunity to see him again. I planned to go to all four nights of the conference, but because of pain from the sciatica I was only able to attend the final night. Yet I truly believed that I was going to be healed again because of the anointing on Randy's life and ministry. Sure enough, the Holy Spirit did funny things with my body while I waited for my turn with Randy. This time I just bounced up and down from my knees for thirty minutes. Then Randy prayed for me, and by the grace of God I was once again healed of all the pain. Glory be to God! I praise His name for His love and mercy.

Kathryn

Back Pain—Lower Left Side

This afternoon, Randy asked those of us who had a word of knowledge to share. There was a young man from Maryland who heard "lower back pain on the left side," which was exactly what I had. It was a re-injury that started two months ago. He prayed for me, and I felt better. In the evening, we went to a church with Bill Johnson. He gave a short sermon, then grew silent, waiting for the Holy Spirit to do His work. After about ten minutes, the entire church, starting from the back row to the front, felt God's strong presence. The Holy Ghost touched many people. About thirty minutes went by, and then Bill asked if there was someone with lower back pain on the left side. That was me! I stood up immediately and checked. The pain was gone completely! Praise the Lord for that! I came here with the heart to serve the Lord, and on the second day God healed me!

Ms. Wong
Global Awakening mission trip to Brazil

Collarbone—Pain and Loss of Mobility from Lump

Tonight I prayed for a woman who had a lump under her collarbone on the right side. The lump caused pain to radiate out into her shoulder as well as stiffness in her joint so she couldn't raise her arm very high, not much past her waist. I asked her when the pain had begun, and she said, "About two or three months ago." I asked if there was anything that she remembered happening in her life around that time, and she said, "No." She also denied any injury to the area. I began commanding the lump to dissolve and disappear and for the pain to go. She then said that the pain was better. Next, I commanded the muscles, ligaments, and tendons to be loosened. I commanded any bone spurs or calcium deposits to be gone. She then stated that the pain was gone and that she was able to lift her arm a little higher than before. I repeated the same prayer and commands after thanking God for what He had already done. I again asked her to raise her arm. She was able to raise it to shoulder level. I repeated the same prayer again, and I commanded full mobility and range of motion to come to her arm. When she tried moving her arm again, she said that there was no pain. She was able to raise her arm above her head and fully rotate her shoulder. Praise God!

Kimberly
Global Awakening mission trip to Australia

Crippled from Birth; Arm and Hand Paralysis

A mother brought her five-year-old son for prayer. He was crippled from birth. His arm and hand were paralyzed. His fingers were completely stiff and bent backward at a forty-five-degree angle. As I knelt beside him, the Holy Spirit poured compassion into my heart for this child. After holding his hand while praying for about five minutes, there was a twitch in his pinky finger. I prayed harder, stopping several times to check his healing progress. I have a young son about his age, and God kept telling me to pray like it was my son. Looking in this child's eyes brought tears to my eyes. The Lord completely healed and restored his arm, hand, and fingers. Hallelujah!

Carey
Global Awakening mission trip to India

Crippled

On Friday evening, we were at El Shaddai Church. During ministry time, the first person brought to me was a young man who was crippled. He could not walk on his own; two others had brought him. They said he had a disease that made him that way. The interpreter could not translate what exactly the disease was, but the problem looked way too big for me. I remember thinking, "God, why have You given me such a difficult one to pray for? I don't have the faith level needed to help this young boy." I began to pray, and he immediately fell down under the power of the Holy Spirit. He began to shake and cry very hard, covering his face with his hands as if he were ashamed for people to see him in this condition.

My compassion for him was overwhelming, and I literally laid myself on top of him and held him while continuing to pray. He was as hot as a furnace, and we both became very sweaty. I didn't realize until later that night, while listening to Randy's message on the angels of healing, that they come like a fire on a person's body. I asked Lucas how he was feeling, and he said he was very hot but he still had a great deal of pain in his legs and feet. I began to pray for his legs, asking God to take away the pain and restore the muscles and tendons to normal. The pain in his legs began to diminish from the top of his legs down. Each time I asked him how the pain was, it seemed like it was moving down his legs very slowly. Finally he only had pain in his feet. The last prayer was for the pain in his feet, and God took that away too. He seemed very exhausted but relieved, and he had a peace about him. I remember thinking, "Thank You, God, for taking away the pain," but I was really disappointed that his full healing had not taken place. I didn't realize that God was still at work in his body. He seemed to be much more pleased with what God had done than I was, and he gave me a big hug. I was really disappointed at myself for having such a lack of faith, especially because there was such a crowd of people around us, watching, waiting, and hoping for the miracle they all wanted to happen. I realized that for me it was a fear-of-man issue. Even though I knew in my heart that this was not about me and was all about God, the enemy was trying to convince me that my faith was not adequate. In spite of my little faith, my compassion for this boy helped me follow through and pray anyway. The rest of the night was wonderful. I watched six people get healed as I prayed for them, and my faith level began to rise.

Then on Thursday evening God finished the rest of the story. I had prayed for many people, several of whom were healed, and then I saw Lucas. He was sitting in the row of chairs in front of me. He had a smile on his face that made him look like an angel. He motioned for me to come to him. He said in broken English, "Do you remember me?" I said, "Yes, of course." It was then that I realized that his chest and stomach were not protruding out in the contorted way that they had previously. "Jesus has healed me," he said. I threw my arms around him and began to weep. He patted me on the back as we hugged as if to say, "It's OK. I understand how you feel." I called for the interpreter. He told her that he was now totally healed. I asked when it happened. He said that God completed the healing process on the following Sunday. He said for me to back up so he could walk to me. I backed up about ten steps, and he walked to me with no difficulty. He still had some distortion in his spine but was much improved. He told us that he had been to the doctor, and it was confirmed that he was healed and it was a miracle. Someone on the team told him earlier in the evening that there was now a healing anointing on him. He said he already knew because Pastor Randy had imparted that anointing to them at the church. We asked if we could stay in touch, and he gave me his e-mail.

I realize that there were probably several of our team members who prayed for him, but I felt privileged to be one of the ones that God chose to start the process of this wonderful healing that has changed the life of this young man. He will now go out and change the lives of countless others as he imparts the healing touch that has been given to him. Like this young man, I too have been changed forever.

Jeff

Global Awakening mission trip to Brazil

Feet—Pain in Big Toes; High Blood Pressure

In the summer of 1994, I was in Saint Paul, Minnesota, to conduct a conference with a group of churches. They had rented a large meeting place, which held around two thousand people. Prior to the conference, I had to attend what turned out to be a contentious meeting, and I was not feeling very compassionate afterward. On top of that, I had been ministering solidly for about twenty-eight days, was exhausted, and was missing my wife and small children. I just wanted to go home. Rather than putting me up in a hotel, my hosts had provided lodging in someone's unfinished basement. The lighting was very poor down there. It reminded me of a dungeon. You had to be very careful how you flushed the toilet to avoid a major plumbing problem. When I went to show the guy who was traveling with me how to flush the toilet, it broke, and water gushed all over the place. As if that wasn't enough, it had been a weird conference. There was a lot of witchcraft going on in the meeting. In the midst of the Holy Spirit moving, a woman dressed in black was sneaking up behind people and dumping cups of cold water on their heads, and we couldn't catch her. Another couple with alcohol on their breath would run up to empty microphones and start cursing.

At the end of the service, I called forward those who wanted to receive the anointing. Fifteen hundred people went to my left, along with seventy-five of the one hundred on our ministry team. The other twenty-five of us were left to pray for the five hundred people who needed healing. I wanted to be with the seventy-five and do the fun "Fill! Fill! Fill!" stuff. I wasn't happy, and my body language was speaking volumes at that point. I was worn out and feeling a distinct lack of compassion. I started down the line praying for people, got to about the fifth guy, and nothing was happening. I was feeling spiritually dry to say the least, and there were about four hundred ninety-five more people to go. Next in line for prayer was a big, old, tall guy. "What is wrong with you?" I asked. "My big toes hurt," he replied. I asked him to take off his shoes and socks, and he did. I knelt down and grabbed hold of one big toe in my right hand and the other big toe in my left hand and began to speak to his toes in the name of Jesus. All of the sudden, it hit me how stupid I must look. I was supposed to be co-laboring with God, but it didn't feel like He was doing His part. Oppression overwhelmed me, along with guilt. All I wanted to do was to go back to the "dungeon" and pull the covers over my head and hide. The enemy was throwing everything and the kitchen sink against me.

I decided it was time for "secret prayer." Secret prayer is prayer so real that it is not permissible to pray out loud because it would cause doubt in everyone around you who might hear it. "Where are You, God?" I prayed. "Why aren't You here? Why have You left me alone? I'm feeling all alone." Suddenly God gave me a vision. He took me back to a time when I was kicked in the head by a horse. I had a horrible fear of horses after that incident. When I was twelve years old, I began to ride again. My dad said to me, "Randy, if that horse throws you, you must get up and get back on, because if you don't get back on, fear will come over you, the horse will sense it, and you will never ride again." I knew exactly what God was saying to me with that vision. I had just been "thrown off" in the healing ministry, and if I didn't continue to press in, I would be too afraid to pray for people ever again. Shame and guilt would overwhelm me, and I would never be effective in the healing ministry. With that, I commenced to pray for the rest of the people in line. The next night, we had people give testimonies of what God did for them on the previous evening. I saw the man with the toe issues from the night before and was on the edge of my seat waiting to hear what happened. When it was his turn, he stepped up to the microphone and said, "I just want to praise God. Last night he healed my high blood pressure!" I was excited for that, but I never did find out if his big toes got healed.

Told by Randy Clark in *The Thrill of
Victory and The Agony of Defeat*

Foot Injury

Before the meeting started, we were praying for those behind the stage. Some people arrived with a man on a stretcher, and we were asked to pray for him. During the interview, we were called away to the front to give words of knowledge. We asked the man if he could wait for us to come back, and he said he would. He had dropped a heavy box on his foot while working for the church. His left foot was bandaged, and we could see fluid leaking through the bandage. He ended up having to wait for over an hour for us to come back and resume praying for him. We wondered if he would still be there, and sure enough, he was. I heard myself ask the Holy Spirit to quicken the process and to come with fire—to start at the top of his head and move down his body to his feet. After some time, he began to laugh really hard and continued to laugh for a long time. Then he jumped up off the stretcher and began to walk. When we asked why he was laughing, he said he was happy. He could feel heat in his head and more down to his foot, and he just knew that God had healed him.

Attendee
Global Awakening mission trip to Brazil

Foot/Ankle Injury

During dinner I noticed that one of the waitresses was limping. I felt that God was telling me to pray for her, but I kept resisting. Dinner finally ended, and I was standing by the door, waiting for my walking partners. God was prompting me again to minister to the waitress so I told Him that if she came out of the kitchen before the group was ready to go, I would pray for her. Just as my fellow walkers came to the door to leave, the waitress came out with some food. On her way back to the kitchen, I stopped her and asked her what was wrong with her foot. She told me that she had tripped earlier at work and hurt her ankle and foot. I explained that I was with a group going around to some churches in New Zealand praying and ministering for people. I asked if she would like me to pray for her ankle. She agreed so I simply asked God to touch her foot, to heal her ankle, and to take away any pain and discomfort. She then tested her foot and could put more weight on it. As she walked a bit, the pain left. She was able to walk normally again. She hugged me and thanked me many times.

As I was walking back to the motel after this experience, I realized that the fear of man almost caused me not to pray for this person's healing. She did not know me and would never see me again so it did not matter if she thought I was a kook. What did matter was whether or not I would obey God. I did obey Him after a few delays and saw my faith increase. Thank You, Lord!

Taraden

Global Awakening mission trip to New Zealand

Foot—Painful Calcium Deposits

Randy taught on words of knowledge and then asked us to come forward and share whatever word we had received. It was my first time standing in front of a meeting of over three hundred people and giving a word of knowledge. I saw a picture in my mind of what looked like a kidney. Then later I got another picture of a kidney being sliced open. When it was my turn, I shared these two pictures, and a man stood up in response. Afterward, he came to me and told me that he donated his kidney to his sister, and today both of them are very healthy. I just said a prayer of blessing over him. Then he told me that his left foot, close to the big toe area, had pain because of calcium deposits. He said the pain was really bad when he had to walk for long periods of time and that this had been going on for years. We laid hands on his foot and prayed, and he said the area felt kind of warm and tingly. We praised God and prayed for more healing and commanded the pain to leave, and it did! Praise Jesus! We both agreed that even though this was not exactly the word of knowledge that I had spoken, God's ways were higher than ours, and it was His will to heal this man.

Winnie
Student
Global Awakening mission trip to Brazil

Finger Pain; Unemployment

An older woman came to me for a problem with her fingers. When she squeezed her hands closed, she had pain in her fingers. After praying several times and rebuking a spirit of affliction, she was totally healed. She also asked for prayer for a job. . Together with the translator, we prayed for a job. The following day, she came up to me and told me that someone called her at 9:30 A.M. that morning and offered her a job. Praise God!

Stacy
Missionary
Global Awakening mission trip to Ukraine

Heel and Leg Pain; Forgiveness

A lady name Marcia came for prayer with pain in her left leg and a lot of pain in her heel. This had been going on for a year. When I asked if anything specific had happened at that time, she said her husband had left her. She admitted that she still had some bad feelings in her heart toward her husband. I led her in a prayer of forgiveness, and she wept.

Then we prayed for her heel, and within seconds she reported that the pain was completely gone.

Dulce
Pastor
Global Awakening mission trip to Brazil

Knee—Torn Meniscus; Mitral Valve Prolapse

I tore the meniscus in my knee, and my doctor said I would need an operation to cut away the torn portion. He operated, and it appeared to be successful. Then during the course of physical therapy, I injured it again. I went back to the doctor, and he said that he would need to remove more of the meniscus and that I would be left partially disabled as a result. I asked him if there was another option, and he suggested a miracle. I went to the Mayo Clinic and got a second opinion, and they concurred. I didn't want another surgery, and I thought that I knew how to get a miracle. I flew out to Bill Johnson's church in California for healing prayer. After that visit, my knee did improve gradually over a period of months.

Then, without knowing how, I injured it again. I did not go back to the doctor because I already knew what he would say. Instead I started fasting and praying. On the thirty-seventh day of my fast, I went to Saint Simon's Island for a church leadership meeting. By this time, my knee was so swollen and painful that I could hardly stand. I heard that Randy Clark was ministering in the next building so I ducked out of my meeting and went to get my knee healed. During the meeting, Randy was talking about how he sensed that God wanted to heal something. He used the example of knee pain as evidence that God wanted to heal a knee. My friend thought that was a word for me, but I was waiting for something more. At the end, Randy called for people with liver problems to come to the front. Because I had a small liver problem, called Gilbert's syndrome, I went for prayer. As the woman prayed for my liver, she started praying over my heart as well. Little did she know that I had three doctors in the past tell me that they had picked up a problem on my EKGs and that I needed to see a heart specialist. I had not gone to the heart specialist at that time. Both my grandfathers died of heart problems, and mitral valve prolapse runs in my family. I figured I did not need to pay a doctor to tell me what I could figure out for myself. As she prayed for my liver and heart, I believed by faith that God was healing them.

Randy then came out into the audience to lay hands on a few people personally. I positioned myself in the group where he was. He walked by me and prayed for some people, and then he returned and walked by me to pray for some others. Then finally he said, "Who is it with the knee problem?" I shouted that it was me, and he kneeled down and laid his hands on my swollen knee. As he prayed, the pain went away and the swelling began to subside. By the time he was done praying, my knee was healed. I could jump and run and dance with no problem. As I walked back to the hotel room that night, the pain started to return. I refused to receive it and commanded it to go, and it did. The next morning, the pain started again, and I commanded it to go—and it did. Since then, I have been pain-free unless I really overdo it. I also went to a cardiologist and had a full workup. They told me I had no sign of any heart problem—no mitral valve prolapse or any other heart problems. All my EKGs since then have been normal.

Cheryl
Saint Simon's Island, Georgia

Knee—Withered Muscles

A young man, approximately twenty years old, stopped me as we were returning to the truck to leave the meeting. He did not speak Portuguese but pointed to his leg. The knee was drawn up, and the foot would not go down to the ground. I put my hand on his knee and prayed a short prayer, asking the power of God to come and restore it. I could feel the muscles around the knee begin to relax and extend. His heel dropped, and the foot lowered to the ground. He put his weight on it cautiously, and when he realized he could stand, he began stomping around with a big smile of delight on his face! Then he did a little dance—really fast—and said something in Makua. The trucks were leaving, and I had to go. This exchange could not have taken more than two and a half minutes, yet it changed his life. Thank You, God, for having me stop for just one more. Thank You for loving on Your son!!

Cindy
Homemaker
Global Awakening mission trip to Mozambique

Knee—Weak Muscles

Here is a testimony from our trip of a twenty-seven-year-old man who had broken his right knee two years ago. The muscles in his leg had become very weak. He had tears in his eyes as he told us he knew Jesus could heal his knee and restore the muscles. I laid my hands on his knee, and he felt heat coming into his knee. The more we prayed, the more he started to sweat from his brow. I had the interpreter ask if his knee and leg were feeling any better. He said, "Fifty percent." I put my hands back on his knee, and he fell out in the Spirit. We continued to pray the anointed healing and fire of Jesus through his whole leg. We brought him back to his feet and asked how the healing was. He said, "One hundred percent." I said, "Let me see." I walked him to the door, and he ran like a young person. He returned and jumped two or three times for joy and to show the strength in his leg. Then he hooked his left foot around his right calf and did a soccer stretch, shifting his knee in a circular motion. The look of joy in his eyes and the praise of glory from his mouth were awesome. I sent him to the back of the stage so they could record his testimony.

Terry
Security Guard
Global Awakening mission trip to Brazil

Knee Pain

A man came up for prayer. We did not have an interpreter so he just pointed to his knee and ankle. We prayed, asking for God's healing, and after a few minutes, we used sign language to see if there was improvement. He indicated "no," and so we prayed again. After a few minutes, we again asked if there had been any improvement. He began to talk to us in Chinese, and this time we were able to find an interpreter to explain to us what he was saying. He told us that he had sinned before he was a Christian, and so he felt that his pain was an attack from the devil. The interpreter had to leave, and so we began to pray again. The man started to cry. We felt that the Holy Spirit showed us that this was not an attack of the enemy, but more the man believing a lie. We prayed in English that God would show this man His truth and bring him joy resulting in the healing of his knee and ankle. The man began to laugh as God touched him, and then he was slain in the Spirit. The group had to leave, and we weren't able to find out if he had been healed. The next morning, the man shared that he had been filled with the Spirit when we had prayed for him. He went home and prayed more that night, and he was filled again; and most of the pain had gone.

Martin
Realtor
Global Awakening mission trip

Knee Pain

Four college students and I were standing talking when a man walked up to us with a cane and said that he had a painful right knee (the students translated for me). I knelt and began to pray for the different parts of his knee. After just a few seconds, I felt pieces of his knee begin to move under his skin. Then I prayed in tongues for about a minute and felt the presence of God. After that, I stood and asked the students how he felt, and they said his response was "perfect." Hallelujah!

Benji

Videographer

Global Awakening mission trip to India

Knee Pain

Will, a carpenter/contractor, had been on his knees all day laying hardwood flooring. His knees were so sore that he had considered not coming to the healing service. As I began to pray for him, I placed my hands on his knees, and those around me laid hands on him too. I prayed for the Holy Spirit to touch him and heal his body. Will started to bend and flex his knees and said that his pain was gone! Praise God!

Team Member

Global Awakening mission trip

Knee Pain

We were at the 26th Quadrangular Church during ministry time. A little girl about eight years old approached me with her father. This was the third consecutive night I had prayed for her. She had undergone an operation on her knee when she was one year old. Never in her life had she been able to run. The first night I prayed for thirty to forty minutes and nothing happened. I left feeling very discouraged. The second night I asked if anything had changed, and her dad said that she had run for the first time. Last night I prayed thirty or forty minutes longer, and he told me the pain had gone away and she could now play like a normal girl! Thank You, Jesus!

Tiffany, age fifteen
Global Awakening Youth Power Invasion trip to Brazil

Lameness

At one point early in the evening, one of the translators found me and asked if I would come and pray for a woman in the back who could not walk. It took us a while to make our way through the crowd, and when we finally reached the back of the room, her friends said that she was not there anymore. While she waited for us to come, the Lord had healed her sovereignly! She had gone off running and jumping and praising God. No one had even prayed for her!

Robbie
Global Awakening mission trip to Brazil

Lameness from Birth; Equilibrium Issues

At the evening meeting, Holy Spirit gave me a word of knowledge that He was going to heal someone who had been born and placed in an incubator. Later that evening, a mother holding her three-year-old son said he was placed in an incubator when he was born and had never walked. I put the boy on the stage and prayed for strength in his legs. Holy Spirit said he had no equilibrium to keep his balance, so in the name of Jesus I commanded his equilibrium to be balanced immediately. Then Holy Spirit said to place him on the ground and to command him to walk. I did this, and he walked without any problem. The mother and other family members, along with me, were in total amazement. This whole process took one to two minutes. Holy Spirit was very specific with the word of knowledge He gave and the things He told me during the prayer time. I had the courage to obey, and instantly the lame boy walked! Praise God!

Jack

District Sales Manager

Global Awakening mission trip to Brazil

Lameness from Birth; Twisted Ankle; Arm Mobility Issues

On Saturday night I prayed for a very sweet ten-year-old girl named Hannah who was in a wheelchair. She was born lame. Her legs were weak and almost totally paralyzed. She also did not have full use of her arms. As we prayed, she prayed along and began to cry. I asked her what she was experiencing, and she said that she was feeling heat in her body. Her mother explained that Hannah had a deep relationship with God and that she often cries when she prays and that God speaks to her. As my interpreter and I prayed, I noticed that she began moving her legs. Then she cried out as God began to touch her. She said that it felt as if someone was pulling and stretching out her legs! I took Hannah by the hands as her parents lifted her out of her wheelchair. I knew God was healing her so I called for another person on the team to help me pray. Lucinda came, and we began praying together for God to increase His healing power. Hannah was so full of faith that she began taking her first steps. Her mom began to cry. I asked if she had ever done that before to make sure that God had indeed done a healing, and her mom said that Hannah had never done anything like that before! Her right ankle, which was slightly twisted, began to straighten. Hannah was so excited as she began moving around. She kept thanking God and saying that He had healed her and that He was going to do more tomorrow!

Clarence

Global Awakening mission trip to Brazil

Lameness; Mental Problems

A seven-year-old girl came up for prayer. Her mother told us that she used a walker or mechanical device to walk and had problems with her brain and her leg muscles. She had never walked on her own. A local pastor and I prayed for release from mental problems, and then we prayed for strength to come into the legs. I asked her if she felt anything, but she hadn't so we prayed again, asking the Lord to bless her with healing in her mind and strength in her legs. She said that she still felt nothing. I then asked her mother if we could ask her to try and walk. She agreed, and I held my arms out; and she took three steps toward me. The smile on her face would have melted a snowman. She then took five steps to her mother and then another five steps to me. Her mother took her up on the stage, and she walked all the way across the stage!

Chad
Software Engineer
Global Awakening mission trip to Brazil

Lameness; Severed Nerves from Surgery

A young lady with braces came up for prayer during the meeting. Her legs were short for her body. She wanted prayer to be able to walk again. Five years prior, she had received an operation to correct a condition, and the surgeon had accidentally severed nerves that kept her from walking without assistance. I laid my hands on her and, wanting to see God glorified, I prayed for "fire," commanding her legs to be healed. I was joined by my wife shortly after and we started walking the girl around the ministry area. She laid down her braces and leaned heavily on us. Her legs were hurting after she walked with our help for about five minutes. We asked her to sit back down in her chair. We prayed some more, and she said her legs felt like they were asleep and there was no pain. We told her that this was good. God was healing her. We then took her by the hands again and commanded her to walk in the name of Jesus. She stood up with no problem and began to walk quickly around the church without any help. This was the first time she had been able to do this in five years. She made several rounds and did this all in high heels! She also received emotional healing for shame and fear. It was awesome. God blessed us all.

Steve
Global Awakening Youth Power Invasion
trip to Curitiba, Brazil

Leg—Length Discrepancy

A young boy, about ten years old, was brought for prayer by his family. He walked with a limp, as one leg was shorter than the other. Without taking off his shoes and socks, I held his feet, and God made his legs the same length. The parents then told me that his legs were twisted. I took off his shoes and socks and pushed up his trouser legs. The lower leg bones were twisted and deformed. I held his feet and legs and prayed. As I prayed, the bones were healed. Due to years of having to compensate, the muscles in one leg were more developed. I prayed a third time, and Doctor Jesus restored the muscles in the weak leg. I had him walk and run with me—totally healed! The boy then sat in the chair with tears of joy on his face as he put his shoes and socks back on. The whole family was crying with joy, and I was too.

Jim
Insurance Sales
Global Awakening mission trip to Brazil

Leg—Left Calf Muscle Withered

The most significant healing I witnessed on this trip was a young man who asked me to pray for his left leg. The muscle of his upper calf was messed up, but as I prayed I could feel God moving the muscle. When

I asked him how he was doing, he indicated that not much had happened and gave me permission to lay my hand on his upper thigh and pray. When I laid my hand on his upper thigh, I discovered that he had almost no muscle. As I prayed, I could feel the muscle regenerate so rapidly that it actually moved my hand. In about twenty seconds, his muscles were back to normal, and he was thrilled, to say the least. It was the first time I had witnessed a creative miracle. God is so good!

John
Pastor
Global Awakening mission trip to Mozambique

Neck—Pain Below Left Ear

Our God is a God of increase. He is able to heal many at the same time. Rob gave a word of knowledge that someone had a pain in the back of the neck, below the left ear. Seven men and a woman came forward and assembled in a group for prayer. Rob asked them if they believed that Jesus could heal them all. As a group, they all agreed that Jesus would heal them all. Everyone held hands, and Rob prayed a simple prayer. In less than a minute, Jesus healed them all! Multiple neck healings! Praise God!

Rob
Home Builder
Global Awakening mission trip to the Middle East

Neck—Pain from Tumor

In 2006, I went on a short-term ministry trip with Global Awakening to India. The first day, we went to a small rural village approximately an hour from Guntur. The church in the village greeted us with wonderful hospitality. At the night meeting, words of knowledge came forth. One of the words given was for pain on the left side of the neck. Soon after, a woman came forward and gave testimony of being healed from a tumor on the left side of her neck. God spontaneously healed her (without human touch or laying on of hands) from a tumor approximately two inches long and half an inch wide. She came to the front of the tent and removed her neck covering. Her neck showed absolutely no trace of tumor, swelling, abnormality, or discoloration. Her pastor, Mr. Paul, saw her neck that night and confirmed that the flesh on her neck was whole. Pastor Paul informed me that it was common knowledge throughout the village that the woman, forty-five years old, had had the tumor her entire life.

Stuart

Social Worker

Global Awakening mission trip to India

Right Side Injury

An elderly lady came up asking for prayer. She had fallen two weeks prior and injured her right side from her shoulder down to her hip. I prayed for healing, and she said she could feel fire going to her right side. She kept checking herself to see if she could raise her arm and if the pain in her hip was gone. After the fifth or sixth time, she could raise her arm in the air, and there was no pain in the hip. I asked for a refreshing for her, and she fell down to the floor very peacefully.

Laurie

Global Awakening mission trip to Auckland, New Zealand

Shoulder Pain—Unable to Raise Arms

I had a word of knowledge about pain in the shoulders causing someone to be unable to raise their arms. When it came time to pray for healing, a man in much pain came up to me and pointed to his shoulders. He could not raise his arms. I started praying for him, and he fell under the Spirit of the Lord. When he got back up and I asked him to test things, he was able to raise his left arm straight above his head with no pain. I asked his name, and he said Louis. We started praying again for more anointing for healing. He could feel heat in both shoulders, and he started moving both shoulders, raising both arms above his head with no pain and saying, "Glory to God. Thank You, Lord" with a tremendous look of joy and gratitude. He had suffered with this for over three years.

Terry
Security Guard
Global Awakening mission trip to Rio de Janeiro, Brazil

Shoulder Pain—Muscle Deterioration

I prayed for a man who was around forty years old. He asked for prayer for his left shoulder. He had pain and limited movement as the result of muscle deterioration that happened when he was twelve years old. Although his arm was fine, the shoulder never recovered. We prayed three to four times. Each time he felt a little better. After the last time, he told me he was healed 100 percent. No more pain! We thanked God!

Adam
Children's Pastor
Global Awakening mission trip to Manaus, Brazil

Sprained Ankle; Sore Wrist

My roommate and I prayed for our hostess the morning we left. She had severely sprained her ankle weeks before and was hobbling the whole time we were there. It had not healed, and I wondered if she had broken it. It was quite swollen, and she could barely walk. We had been shopping the day before, and she had to go to the car because of the pain. She couldn't be on the foot for long because of the pain. I told her that God wanted to heal her, but she said she had prayed and God hadn't healed her. She had been prayed for several times and had not been healed. She took the attitude with me that if God was going to heal her, He would have done it already. She had a sore wrist along with the sprained ankle. My roommate, Laurie, prayed for her wrist, and God healed it. Then we prayed for her ankle and told her to test it. God completely healed her ankle. She started walking and saying, "That's amazing. There is no pain. That is amazing." The thing is, I don't think she truly believed she was going to be healed because she had already been prayed for several other times. It just goes to show you that we need to continue to receive prayer because we never know when God is going to show His glory and do a miracle or healing on our behalf. This testimony shows the power of perseverance. Yes, God is amazing!

Cristina

Global Awakening mission trip to Australia

Torn Hamstring

A young man came for prayer for a torn hamstring in his left leg. We prayed, and the pain instantly left him. The knot in his muscle also softened and disappeared. Praises!

Kenton

Pastor

Global Awakening mission trip to Brazil

Torn Tendons and Ligaments

On the last night of our meetings, a large man asked me to pray for his right leg that had been injured in a motorcycle accident. He told my interpreter that all the tendons and ligaments in his leg had been torn and that he was scheduled to have surgery to repair the damage. I anointed him with oil and began calling on the Lord to release His healing power. I then put both hands around his leg and prayed that God would restore and repair the damage. I commanded the ligaments and tendons to be made whole in Jesus's name. Immediately, I began to feel vibrating in my hands, and as I blessed what God was doing, the anointing increased. It was as if I could feel guitar strings vibrating in my hands at an incredible speed as God performed the surgery and repaired his leg. He began to cry and shake as he felt the power of God healing him. Then my interpreter said he saw a bright light shoot into his leg as all three of us fell to the ground under God's anointing and power. We lay on the ground in total amazement, crying, praising, and thanking God for the miracle we were experiencing. We were finally able to stand, and I asked him to do something he hadn't been able to do since the accident. He tried to jump and said it was much better, but there was a small amount of pain on one side so I told him we were going to pray again and ask God to complete the surgery. Once again, I put my hands around his leg. This time it felt like a ping-pong ball bouncing around in my hands as he fell to the ground. I could hardly believe what God was allowing me to experience. When he got up the second time, I asked him to try again to do something he could not do. He jumped in the air, came down, and felt no pain, then took off running up and down the aisle, crying in total amazement. (He was unable to run or jump prior to his surgery by "Doctor Jesus.") I told him to remember to thank God every day for his healing and to be a testimony for the Lord. I have had the privilege of praying for the sick many times, and God has miraculously healed many. But I had never physically felt God perform surgery right in my hands while praying. My faith has soared, and I thank my Lord for allowing me to have such an incredible experience of His healing power! My life will never be the same!

Dave

Global Awakening mission trip to Brazil

NERVOUS SYSTEM

The NERVOUS SYSTEM consists of the nerves of the body, including the nerves of the brain and spinal cord, the nerves of the peripheral nervous system (the thoracic nerves, the lumbar nerves, the lumbosacral plexus nerves, and the nerves of the autonomic nervous system), the cranial nerves, and the eyes and ears and their major nervous pathways.

Then will the eyes of the blind be opened and the ears of the deaf unstopped. Then will the lame leap like a deer, and the mute tongue shout for joy.
—ISAIAH 35:5-6

Astigmatism

At one of our services, I had a mother and son come up for prayer. She wanted prayer for her son's height and his eyes. He was fourteen years old and short for his age. Cheri proceeded to ask some questions such as, "How tall do you want to be?" Then we prayed for him, and she spoke over him and stated that by the age of eighteen he would reach his desired height. We also prayed for his eyes. He had astigmatism and couldn't see up close to read. I heard the Lord telling me to put my hands on his eyes, and so I did and started to pray. Cheri added more to the prayer. We checked to see if there was healing, and there was. We prayed more. We then had him read my nametag and the back of our little cheat paper with Portuguese words that were quite small. He could see up close now and was able to read the words. He was 100 percent healed! Tears flowed down his face. Wow, God is so awesome and loving!

Penny
Homemaker
Global Awakening mission trip to Brazil

Back Pain—Nerve Damage from Childbirth

I wasn't thinking of getting prayer for my back when I went to the conference. It had been so long (thirty-eight years), and I was so accustomed to the pain (also drained from it) and had had so much prayer that I had just learned to live with it. I really didn't have any faith left for a healing in this area, but when it came time for prayer, I felt led to go ahead and ask Randy to pray. Although I was both hopeless and exhausted from the pain, which wiped me out physically and mentally, at that moment I suddenly felt hope for the first time, and I didn't know why.

My problem started after the birth of my second child, when I felt something tear in my back during delivery. It was worse than pain. It was an extreme sensitivity that felt like something was rubbing against exposed nerves at the base of my spine, sending a terrible, hyper-intolerable sensation throughout my body that prevented me from sleeping, thinking, praying, or doing anything at all except trying to find a way to stop it. If even a feather touched my back, it would send me through the roof with awful nerve sensations. It's very difficult to explain, and no doctor was ever able to figure it out. One opinion was that the myelin sheath covering the nerves was torn, leaving them exposed. Another theory was that a nerve might be imbedded in scar tissue from the tear, or that a nerve was touching a protruding disc. No one could give me a definitive diagnosis, and so there was no remedy. Randy said he had a word some years before that the Lord was healing women's bodies from damage done in childbirth, and so he prayed that for me.

I didn't have any sensation at all except for the unbelievable amount of love and concern I felt from Randy as he prayed. He had a long line waiting, and yet he took a lot of time with me, allowing me to feel the Lord's personal care. I have never forgotten it. While I had no immediate relief, the next day I noticed it was getting better; and by the end of the week or so, I felt almost totally free of pain. I gave a testimony at our church because I knew it was gone. When I say "knew," I don't mean by faith; I mean by the absolute lack of tenderness and sensitivity in my back.

So as not to diminish what happened, I feel you need to know the rest of the story. The healing lasted two to three years. I could sit comfortably in chairs, and I could bend, stretch, reach, etc., without setting it off. But when a very emotionally painful situation occurred, it came back—worse than ever. I stood on God's Word, had lots of prayer, and wished I could find Randy! Again I went to the doctors, hoping they would figure out what was going on, but they could not. Then a physical therapist told me that stress always attacks our weak places. Armed with that knowledge, I started to reclaim my healing. I am now making great progress and feel the Lord is moving me along. I am learning as I go. This is the important part—I did not lose my healing after Randy prayed. I was attacked in a formally weak area. More importantly, the healing I received through the beautiful care and sincerity that I experienced when Randy prayed for me has never faded. I know it was the Lord working through Randy, and I am so very grateful for his obedience. I really hope you will count my story as worthwhile because it is amazing—thirty-eight years and suddenly, out of the blue, in the middle of my lack of faith, or even hope, God healed me. It still amazes me.

Pam
Global Awakening conference

Back Pain—Possible Spinal Cord Damage from Anesthesia; Forgiveness

A woman requested prayer for her back. She previously had surgery, and the place where the anesthesia had been applied had suffered nerve damage. She was having trouble sitting through the meetings and would experience pain after standing for an hour. I asked her if she had any unforgiveness. She said that she had been hurt by a church leader who severely chastised her for something she did. She prayed to forgive that person, then we prayed for healing, and all pain was gone. I asked her to come back to us during the breaks to let us know if she was still pain-free. She returned several times and reported that she had no pain!

Sherry
Missionary
Global Awakening mission trip to China

Back and Shoulder Pain—Sciatic Nerve Pain; Emotional Wounding

A twenty-two-year-old woman came forward for prayer. She was suffering from pain from a bike/car accident two years ago. Her spinal column was exerting pressure on her sciatic nerve, causing pain, and she was experiencing pain in her shoulder from the same accident. I asked God's Spirit to come, and she began to shake and tremble. I continued praying and, in a few minutes, asked her to check her pain. It was 100 percent gone in her back and shoulder. Still shaking, she began to express sorrow in her face. The Lord spoke to my heart about an emotional wounding she had suffered. I held her close in my arms and asked God to let her experience His love. I kissed her head and let her cry on and on. When she was done, she shared that she had asked God to send someone to hold and kiss her, but she didn't expect that He would send someone all the way from the United States.

Cindy
Homemaker
Global Awakening mission trip to Argentina

Bleeding from One Ear

A lady came to the meeting with her husband because she wanted to see if God was real and if He could heal her. She didn't tell anyone about her condition other than her husband. Her reasoning was, "If God is real, He will heal me without me telling anyone what is wrong." When she came up for prayer, for some reason I didn't ask her what she wanted prayer for. Instead I just prayed peace and love over her. I learned later that she had been bleeding from one ear for a year without stopping. She went to sleep that night and woke up at 12:00 A.M. with no bleeding. She again woke up at 9:00 A.M. and still no bleeding. Her husband went to their pastor's house early in the morning and woke him up, testifying how Jesus healed his wife.

John
Global Awakening mission trip to Brazil

Blind in One Eye

At a church in Medellín, Brazil, a man came forward for prayer for his blind eye. He had a disease that had caused the blindness. He could see light, but that was all. We prayed four times without any change, and the man was ready to leave. I told him to have faith, that I had seen this happen many times and that we should keep praying because I believed God would heal him. We prayed again, and this time God restored some vision to his eye. We kept praying, and God kept restoring his vision until he could see as good out of that eye as the other one. Praise God!

Builder from Alabama
Global Awakening mission trip to Brazil

Blind Left Eye; Dead Cornea

About twelve weeks ago, we started a healing class that was to meet every Friday night using Randy Clark's training manual. The first night there were only two of us. We decided that one of us would pretend to have a shoulder problem and the other would pray using the five-step prayer model from the manual. When I got home that night, the church called and said that a lady had been brought in who was blind in her left eye. The cornea was completely dead, and they were going to operate on it on Monday. The doctor had told her that he was going to cut the cornea out and replace it with a cadaver's eye. She did not want the surgery. Seven of us assembled and prayed for her. The following Monday, when she went to the doctor, he was amazed to find that there were new blood vessels in the dead area of her eye. He wanted to know what had happened. He said he had never seen a dead cornea improve, let alone grow new blood vessels. Even though the blood vessels were growing, she still could not see. She has kept coming to our healing class for prayer, and little by little her eyesight is being restored.

Bill

Blindness; "Spit in Her Eyes"— an Act of Obedience

In 1995, I was able to raise a large sum of money to take with me to Russia for a conference. With this money I was able to pay the hotel expenses for a thousand pastors and church planters who had come to the conference. On my team was a Vineyard pastor. He had been praying for an older Russian woman who was basically blind. Even if she held a Bible two inches from her face she could just barely read it. In the course of praying for this woman, the Lord told the pastor to spit in her eyes and He would heal her.

This Vineyard pastor came to me and told me this and then asked me what I thought he should do. He was submitting to me as the leader of the team. My response was to have him ask her if she was comfortable with him spitting in her eyes, and if so, then do it. When he asked her, she said, "Yes. Spit!" So he spit in his hands and rubbed it in her eyes, and her eyes opened immediately. By asking her permission, we were allowing her to make the decision, and then we were able to come into agreement with her for her healing.

Told by Randy Clark in his sermon "Acts of Obedience"

Blindness; Pain in Side

A woman brought a man (a relative) who was blind, epileptic, and had a pain in his side. Great woman of faith that I am (ha!) I prayed first for the pain in the side. The pain left right away, and we rejoiced and thanked God. We were standing close to the speakers, and it was so loud that as I began to pray for his eyes, I just prayed in tongues. As I prayed, I was thinking to myself, "He's blind, and there are a lot of people waiting for prayer. I'll just pray quickly and go on because I could pray for hours for him and maybe something would happen and maybe not!" I prayed in tongues no more than five minutes and went on to the next person. All of a sudden, there was a big commotion next to me! I asked my translator what was going on. She had an incredulous look on her face because he could see! His family was all around him, rejoicing. The woman who brought him was in tears, rejoicing and praising God! Then the man went to each relative and told them what they were wearing. His healing elevated the faith of all those around him. The people now were more expectant than ever to be healed, and I too expected the Lord to heal them. The Lord totally healed all but two of the twenty-some people I prayed for!

Marcia
Homemaker
Global Awakening mission trip to Brazil

Blindness; Ankle/Foot Pain; Achilles Tendon; Diabetes; Deafness

A woman came to us and asked for prayer for her eyes. She was 100 percent blind in her right eye and partially blind in the other. I started to pray, and she was able to see light and shapes. All of a sudden, my translator told me that this woman's foot had also just been 100 percent healed! Five years ago she had her Achilles tendon removed, and she couldn't walk without excruciating pain. Now the pain was completely gone without anyone praying for it. The next night she came back. She told me she had diabetes. When I prayed for that, God's fire came on her strongly. She was red and sweating all over. Her eyes also got a little bit better. The next night she came back with her husband. He was 100 percent deaf in his left ear, and God totally restored his hearing. Then

God touched the lady, and her vision was totally healed. She had perfect vision, and her heart was so happy. Praise God!

Erin
Global Awakening Youth Power Invasion
trip to Curitiba, Brazil

Blind Right Eye

During the afternoon ministry time, an elderly lady (about fifty to sixty-five years old) named Julvia (her name means "glory") asked for prayer. She indicated that she had been blind in her right eye for more than ten years. I could see the stigma in the eye that had caused the blindness. She could not read anything on my nametag. As I prayed for her, the power of the Holy Spirit hit her. She was weeping out of her right eye. When she opened her eyes, she could read my nametag perfectly with her left eye covered. Praise the Lord!

John
Insurance and Investment Sales
Global Awakening mission trip to Brazil

Blind Right Eye

I prayed for a lady who had no vision in her right eye. I could see that her eye was not focusing. I told her to put her hand over that eye, and I put my hand over her hand and prayed for God to touch her eye. She fell out in the Spirit and began crying. Then I prayed for peace of mind for her. When she got up, we (my translator and I) asked what amount of vision had returned. She said she could see a little better, and then she cried, "I can see completely!" I think the healing was taking place as we talked. She touched my hair and said she could read the banners; then she began to cry, and joy came over her face. I noticed that her eye was now focused. She gave me a big hug, and off she went.

Tonya
FDA Investigator
Global Awakening mission trip to Londrina, Brazil

Blind Right Eye from Aneurism; Headache

A woman brought her seventy-two-year-old mother named Maria for prayer. Maria had suffered an aneurism, resulting in loss of vision in her right eye. Maria said that she had pain in the center of her brain, so I prayed first for her brain, and shortly afterward the pain left her. I then laid my hands over her eyes. Gradually, her left eye became clearer, and her right eye could see light and the outline of images. I continued to pray, and Maria could then see the pin stripes in her translator's tie. She smiled at me as she looked into my eyes and told me that we had the same color eyes and that she could see 100 percent now! The Lord was gracious in allowing me to pray for Maria's blind eye. What a wonderful Lord we serve who gladly restores sight to the blind!

Neil
Global Awakening mission trip to Rio de Janeiro, Brazil

Blind Right Eye

A little boy who was completely blind in his right eye was brought to us for prayer. Another member of my team had prayed for him four times with no healing and was frustrated. They had asked him how he became blind, and he said he didn't know. However, when I asked him, he said that his brother had kicked him in the eye a year ago and he had been blind since. I immediately asked him if he would forgive his brother, and he did. I prayed for him and then covered his good eye and asked him to tell me how many fingers I was holding up. He got it right the first time! The Lord restored his vision! Hallelujah!

Amy, age eighteen
Global Awakening Youth Power Invasion
trip to São Paulo, Brazil

Carpal Tunnel Syndrome

During one of the services, God healed a man of carpal tunnel syndrome. He had great pain and no strength in his hands. After God healed him, he could grip my hands firmly. I put pressure on his wrists to test it, and he smiled because there was no more pain.

Builder from Alabama
Global Awakening mission trip to India

Cataracts; Eye Damage

A middle-aged male pastor was healed of cataracts on his right eye. He also was healed of damage that affected the way his eye opened as a result of a botched surgery.

Maude
Retired Teacher and Seminary Student
Global Awakening mission trip to China

Cataracts

A young woman came to me for prayer for her eyes. She had been diagnosed with cataracts, and her struggle to see was causing great pain, especially behind her temples. She said that when she looked at us, we were "fuzzy and blurry." I placed my hands on her temples and then on her eyes; then I asked the Lord to relieve the pain and restore her sight. There was some improvement. We prayed again, and this time when she opened her eyes, they were bright and clear! She looked at my interpreter's nametag and actually read the fine print at the top that said, "Lighting Fires, Casting Visions, and Building Bridges." She didn't understand what she was reading, but she could read the words. Hallelujah! This was my very first prayer experience in Brazil!

Karen

Registered Nurse

Global Awakening mission trip to Brazil

Cataracts; Hearing Loss; Back and Knee Pain; Arthritis in Hands

On our last night in Brazil, a lady brought her elderly mother for prayer. She was sixty-eight years old but looked and acted much older. She needed a major overhaul! Her cataracts were so bad that she was legally blind. She was so deaf that her daughter had to scream in order for her to hear. She had major problems with her back and knees, causing her great pain. I started by praying for her eyes. After a quick, simple prayer asking God to remove the cataracts, she opened her eyes, looked around, and began crying. She could see perfectly! I then prayed another quick and simple prayer for God to heal her ears. Immediately she could hear perfectly. Her daughter tested her by standing behind her and whispering. She heard every word! I then asked my assistant/interpreter to pray for her back and knees. Before praying, we asked her to bend over to see what she could do. She grimaced in pain as she leaned slightly over and could barely bend her knees without pain. After a quick and simple prayer asking God to heal her, the woman immediately bent all the way over and was able to touch her feet with her hands. She then did two deep knee bends. Everyone standing around was amazed, especially my assistant/interpreter, who was in shock. Then to top it all off, she asked for prayer for her hands. Her arthritis was so bad that her knuckles were stiff and she couldn't close here hands. Again, my assistant prayed a quick, simple prayer, and the woman was healed at once! She started closing her hands, making a fist, and hitting her other hand. She and her daughter were overcome with joy, and we were all blown away! The church erupted in praise as she testified of what God had done for her. That's the first time I've ever seen someone with that many problems get healed of all of them on the first prayer each time. It was truly amazing to see what God did. I felt no anointing, nothing as we prayed. God did it all!

Gary and Kathi
Global Awakening mission trip to Vitória, Brazil

Crossed Eyes

Tonight, I went with part of the team to a Foursquare church. Nilesh was preaching and asked me to translate. When we got into the church, he saw two angels; one of them was at the corner playing a harp, and the other one came like a flash of light. During the words of knowledge, someone said "cross-eyed." We hadn't prayed yet, but I saw a little girl in front of us who took off her glasses and started to weep. When we asked people to give their testimonies, this little girl, who was maybe six or eight years old, came to the front and said she was the one who had crossed eyes and she also couldn't see clearly with her right eye. God healed her eyes!! It was so exciting! When the service finished, a lady came to me and told me that her little son saw a light over my head while I was translating the sermon. The whole night was supernatural!

Rebecca, age nineteen
Global Awakening Youth Power Invasion
trip to Curitiba, Brazil

Deaf from Birth

Ministry time started off with a huge push toward the front of the stage as God began touching people. I found myself surrounded by a multitude of people, all wanting more of God. I began praying for a seventeen-year-old girl who had never had the ability to hear. She could read lips, but not very well. I interviewed her and found out that she had the ability to talk but had never learned to speak because she could not hear audible sounds. We came against this spirit of deafness with tremendous faith for her healing. The Lord began to instruct me to pray against the lie of the enemy, which had convinced this girl that she was never going to hear. When we prayed those words, we instantly saw 30 percent of her hearing restored. Our faith meter began to increase, and we plunged in for more prayer before the Throne. Another five to ten minutes passed, and another 20 percent increase in hearing occurred. The girl was beginning to get really excited, and you could see her countenance brighten. She now had 50 percent of her hearing so we went for the rest. Soon she was turning her head at every sound around her, which frightened her a bit because she hadn't heard these sounds before. We brought her before the leadership of the church, and they interviewed her and put her through a couple of confirming exercises. She passed them all 100 percent!

Brian
Sales
Global Awakening mission trip to Goiânia, Brazil

Deaf from Birth

On Friday night, we had the first of the crusade meetings at a soccer stadium. My wife, Victoria, and I went under one of the tents when it began to rain. After the rain stopped, one of the trip coordinators said, "Go find some sick people, and pray for them." As it turned out, we were in the "healing tent" so we didn't have to look for sick people. They were all around us. We spent the next three and a half to four hours in a space about five feet by five feet, praying for those who came to us. Here is one of the significant healings we witnessed: A Brazilian woman came up to us with a little nine-year-old girl. Through our interpreter, we found out that the little girl had been born deaf. As we started to pray, the compassion of God for this little one was poured into my heart. I knelt down in front of her and took both of her hands in mine and began crying so hard that I could not even speak. Victoria started praying and asking for healing for her ears. After a few minutes, Victoria asked the mother if she would communicate to the little girl and see if anything was happening. The mother bent down and started asking the little girl questions, and the little girl's eyes got real wide because she could hear her mother speaking. Our interpreter said, "She can hear!" Victoria looked at the interpreter and said, "Are you sure?" "Yes, she can hear," she replied! God healed a nine-year-old girl on Friday night out of His love and compassion. It was amazing!

Barry

Engineer

Global Awakening mission trip to Brazil

Deaf and Mute from Birth

I was praying for people in a crowd of about three thousand to four thousand people when I noticed a man pointing to his ears and mouth. At first, I thought he was referring to himself. But as I moved closer, I saw that he wanted me to pray for a girl who looked like she was about ten years old. The man motioning me to pray for her was her pastor and had brought her to the meeting. He told me she had been born deaf and did not speak. After interviewing further, I began to pray. Having prayed for several deaf people who had been healed, I thought this might take a half hour to one hour. To my surprise, I had prayed for about five minutes when the girl looked as if she might be starting to hear. I snapped my fingers in her ears, and she seemed to hear. She could read lips so I told her to raise a hand when she heard anything—left hand for left ear, right hand for right ear, and both for both ears. As I snapped my fingers, she accurately raised the appropriate hand or hands. Realizing that sometimes a person can hear a snap but not be able to hear other tone levels, I stepped behind her and began to make sounds at different levels of the music scale. Again, she accurately raised her hands. I was happy and surprised all at the same time that her healing had happened so quickly—probably in less than five minutes. Excitement filled her face, and her pastor was crying for joy. I next began to call her by name and was overjoyed as I saw her listen to the sound of her own name and then other words like "Jesus" and "Obrigado," which means "I am obliged," or "thank you," in Portuguese. I will never understand the ministry of healing. I know one thing: it isn't my power or me. I thank God that I get to see these miracles happen. Thank You, Jesus. Thank You, Holy Spirit. Thank You, Father.

Randy Clark
Global Awakening mission trip to Goiânia, Brazil

Deaf in Both Ears

A man named Flavio came forward for prayer as a result of a word of knowledge. He was seventy years old and deaf in both ears. Before anyone prayed for him, he received partial hearing in both ears simply from the word of knowledge. He asked me to pray for full restoration of his hearing. After placing my hands on his ears and stating, "Ears be healed in Jesus's name. Let Your anointing oil flow," Flavio said he could hear more clearly. He closed his eyes, and we prayed again; and his hearing improved greatly this time. I tested it by standing about a foot away from each ear and clicking my fingers. He raised his hand when he heard the sound. I continued to step further away while clicking my fingers, and, with his eyes closed, Flavio kept acknowledging he could hear. I ended up a good fifteen feet away from him. He could now hear quite well, but there was a sizzling or cracking sound going on in his ears. I commanded the sizzle to leave in the name of Jesus and for complete clarity of hearing to come. He opened his eyes. I stepped back about ten feet and spoke to him, and he could hear perfectly with no sizzling or cracking. More amazing is that Flavio understood what I was saying (in English). Thank You, Jesus!

Brian
Technology Management
Global Awakening mission trip to Brazil

Deaf in Both Ears

During one of the healing services, Joe, a missionary, brought a man named Luis to me for prayer. Two years prior, Luis had died and been resuscitated in the hospital but lost all hearing in both ears. Prior to this, his hearing had been normal. Luis had a dream in which he heard the name "Randy Clark." He had never heard of me before in the natural. He saw me in the dream; and in the dream, I had prayed for him, and he was healed. Then, in the dream, I laid hands on him, and he received a healing anointing.

When I first started praying for Luis, nothing happened. I stuck my fingers in his ears, commanding the spirit of deafness to get out, but it didn't leave. Yet because of the dream, I believed he was going to receive his healing and it was going to happen that night. I snapped my fingers around his ears as I continued to press in for healing. The weighty presence of God came on him, and he went down on the floor as I continued commanding him to hear. I started saying, "I believe you are going to hear." Then, when I spoke his name, he moved his head toward me. I spoke his name again, and he opened his eyes. I said, "You are hearing me, aren't you?" and he replied, "Yes, I can hear everything you are saying." It was a very exciting healing—a real divine setup!

Randy Clark
Global Awakening mission trip to Brazil

Deaf in Both Ears

I prayed for an older man who was deaf in both ears. He did have a hearing aid in his left ear. After praying once that his ears would be opened, he could hear a little better. I prayed again more specifically that the tubes and parts of his ears would be reconnected, and one ear was completely healed! I prayed again, asking God to reconstruct the nerves, and he was healed 100 percent! He took his hearing aid out and talked easily with the interpreter. Praise God!

Connie
Global Awakening mission trip to Londrina, Brazil

Deaf in Left Ear from Birth

A young woman came for prayer. She had had 90 percent hearing loss in her left ear since birth. I shared with her how God healed me of an incurable disease and that Vanessa, the interpreter, and I believed God was going to heal her left ear that night. She too believed God was going to heal her. Placing my hand on her ear, I prayed for God's Holy Spirit to come with His healing power and for His angels to remove what was causing this hearing loss. I removed my hand, and she said she could hear a little better. I told her this was very good because God was working and we were going to continue praying until total hearing was restored. I prayed two more times, and she was 100 percent healed. We praised God together. She cried, and I held her. I felt led to pray for God to fill her with His peace and all the fruits of the Spirit. What a mighty God we serve! We give God all the glory and honor due to His holy name.

Many Ann
House Cleaning Business
Global Awakening mission trip to Londrina, Brazil

Deaf in Left Ear

A middle-aged woman presented herself for prayer for deafness in her left ear. She had about 80 percent hearing loss in the ear. We prayed for a few minutes, and her hearing became better. Judy would periodically whisper in her left ear. Her eyes told us everything. The more her hearing improved, the more "engaged" she became. After a time of prayer, her left ear opened completely and she heard perfectly! Praise the Lord Jesus Almighty! His precious blood shall never lose its power!

Rob—Home Builder

Judy—Realtor

Global Awakening mission trip to Londrina, Brazil

Deaf in Right Ear; Back Pain

A grey-haired man in his seventies came for prayer for back pain and a deaf right ear. First I prayed for the back pain. My right hand was shaking. He grabbed my hand and held on to it for dear life, and then he began to shake all over. As I placed my left hand over his right ear, he became very still, as if paralyzed. Finally, I asked him what had happened. He said it felt like a bolt of lightning had struck him. We covered his ear and asked if he could hear from the right ear. "Yes," he cried, "I can hear, and my back pain is gone." He lifted his hands, praising God. Hallelujah. Glory. Praise God!

Bob

Retired

Global Awakening mission trip to Rio de Janeiro, Brazil

Deaf in Right Ear; Blindness; Headaches

This was an explosive night of healings. Randy prayed corporately for healing, which resulted in widespread healings for those present, with almost every person in attendance waving their hands in the air testifying to Jesus Christ's healing power. The Spirit of the Lord was definitely present for healing. As the team went out among the crowd, we prayed for those who had not yet received healing or who had a second and third condition. I had two translators with me, one on each side, interviewing people to determine what they wanted prayer for. I felt like this was the New Testament all over again as the crowds pressed in just to receive a touch. We came to a boy about thirteen years old who was completely deaf in his right ear from birth. He couldn't hear at all when I snapped my finger in that ear. We prayed for about two minutes, and his eyes fluttered; and when I snapped in his ear again, he communicated that it had completely opened. He then quickly turned around and walked away. I remember not believing that he was healed because it happened so quickly. Before he walked away, I made my translator ask him a few times if he was totally healed. She couldn't believe that I didn't believe he was healed. He left with great joy. That same night, I saw another deaf ear open, and one completely blind eye and two almost blind eyes made well. Things happened so fast that I don't recall every healing. It was all just a blur. It was amazing to see how many people had headaches. There were so many, and they were healed so quickly— I only took about a minute praying for each one. I just started touching them quickly, rebuking the pain, and they were all healed in seconds. I think because of the large number of people and the great need, God just didn't waste any time.

Brian
Student
Global Awakening mission trip to India

Deaf in Right Ear; Spirit of Rejection

We were up on a hill interceding for the morning session when a woman came to us. She was deaf in her right ear. We began to pray, when Tanja got an impression of a goat. We also received words of knowledge about "rejection" and "low self-worth," and Laurie heard "scapegoat." We shared these words with the woman, and upon receiving them, she fell out in the Spirit. We prayed God's love and original design in her life and for a creative miracle—that God would go in and heal the broken parts. After we broke off the spirits of deafness and affliction, we prayed for God's living water to come, and then we sprinkled water in her ear. Wanting to see if she was healed, her mother spoke sentences in her ear, and she was able to repeat them, which she hadn't been able to do before.

Merril—Student
Tanja—Marketing Coordinator
Laurie—Affordable Housing Developer
Global Awakening mission trip to China

Deaf in Right Ear from Birth

My friend and I prayed for a woman who had been deaf in her right ear since birth. We prayed for a good hour, and she said it was 90 percent better! Then we asked God for 100 percent healing, and I got the feeling that we needed to sing over her ear. We sang, and about five minutes later, her ear was 100 percent opened! She was so amazed she couldn't even talk! Thank You, Jesus!

Laura
Office Manager
Global Awakening Youth Power Invasion
trip to São Paulo, Brazil

Deaf in Right Ear from Infection

At the end of the message, after many had been healed through God's gift of words of knowledge, Jamie, the intern/preacher, asked those who wanted prayer to come forward. A lady named Rachel, age thirty-five, came forward, and as she approached you could see and feel the power of the Holy Spirit on her. She almost went to the floor under the power of God. One of her ears was bright red. She said that two years ago, an infection had left her totally deaf in her right ear. As we began to pray, the presence and power of God came on her, and she said she felt a zap of electricity from her tailbone to her ear. With that, she fell to the floor. After about five minutes, we asked if she was able to hear any better, and she responded, "No." We started praying again, and as I placed my fingers just below the ear, I felt muscles twitching. Ten minutes later, she got up with the biggest surprised look on her face and said, "I felt God pull the deafness out of my ear, down my spine, and out the tailbone, much like the same path that the zap took. I now hear perfectly." She got so excited that the power of God hit her again, and she fell out on the floor. Right ear deaf for two years—100 percent healed. Praise God!

Van
Senior Pastor
Global Awakening Youth Power Invasion
trip to Curitiba, Brazil

Deafness; Muteness

On the last night of the crusade, a woman brought her deaf and mute teenage daughter to me for prayer. I was mobbed as people reached out from all sides so I asked the Holy Spirit to move with mercy and compassion since there were so many people in need. I then placed my hands on the girl's ears and mouth and commanded the deaf and dumb spirit to leave in Jesus's name. Afterward, I asked her to say, "Ahh." She opened her mouth wide, but no sound came out. I continued to press in, asking the Lord for mercy and compassion. I asked her again to say, "Ahh." When she did say, "Ahh," speaking for the first time in her life, excitement filled the air. Everyone around was amazed at what God had done. Tears of joy filled her mother's eyes as the young girl continued to repeat, "Jesus! Hallelujah!" I took her to the platform to give her testimony so that others would know what an awesome God we serve. To God be the glory! Thank You, Lord!

Hyacinth

Global Awakening mission trip to India

Deafness; Muteness

A mother brought her twelve-year-old son for prayer. He was deaf and dumb from birth. We prayed for him, and after three to four minutes, he looked up and smiled, indicating he could hear a little. As we continued to pray, he made a sound as he tried to speak. A big smile crossed his face as he heard himself speak for the first time. His mother cried, and I cried; and then the three of us shouted out the name of Jesus over and over. Praise the Lord!

Art

Pastor

Global Awakening mission trip to India

Deafness; Muteness; Lameness

A mother came to us carrying her son in her arms. I think the boy was about four years old. He had been born four months prematurely and had never spoken, never heard, and never walked. Immediately, when the translator told me this, I knew he was going to walk. I absolutely believed because God gave me a gift of faith. I took the boy in my arms and just hugged him for maybe ten to twenty seconds and didn't say a word. I just closed my eyes and turned my heart to God and believed in Ephesians 2:6, which says we are seated in heavenly places. I didn't ask God for anything. Then the Holy Spirit told me to put the boy on the ground. When I did, he immediately ran up the stairs to the pulpit. He had the biggest smile on his face because he was walking for the first time in his life. I couldn't catch him for a while to pray for his ears and mouth because he didn't want to stop running! I was finally able to place my hands on his ears and mouth and command, in the name of Jesus, that they would be opened. Five minutes later, the microphone turned on and we heard, "Da Da" from the little boy who had never said anything before! The family left before we could find out about his ears, but I believe his hearing was also restored that day.

Timothy
Global Awakening mission trip to Brazil

Deafness—Many Healed; Tinnitus; Forgiveness

Tonight's teaching was on the power of the testimony, and I was invited to give a testimony about the healing of a deaf man. When ministry time began, Tom instructed everyone with hearing problems to line up to receive prayer from me. The line was long. One by one, the interpreter and I prayed for them. There were so many it was difficult to remember the details, but I'll try. Two of the men in the line each had tinnitus, characterized by a continuous ringing in the ears. Both were touched mightily by God's manifest presence and felt they were healed, but they had to wait until they were in a quiet place to know with certainty. One man's ear was not healed until unforgiveness was discovered and dealt with. When he was able to forgive, all it took was one quick prayer and he was healed. He was even more grateful for his newfound inner peace than he was for the healing of his deaf ear. After that, we prayed for six people in a row who were totally deaf or mostly deaf in their left ear. Every one of them had their hearing restored. A middle-aged woman had been deaf in one ear and had very little hearing in the other. Her deaf ear was opened, and the other had dramatic improvement. If you could have seen the look on her face, your heart would have leaped for joy, as mine did.

Attendee
Global Awakening mission trip to Brazil

Dyslexia

She came to me with a severe case of dyslexia. She was reading at a second-grade level but was in the eighth grade. When I prayed for her, she went out in the Spirit and rested on the floor. While she was resting in the Spirit, she had a vision of angels coming and opening the top of her skull and rewiring her brain. When she got up off the floor, she told her parents about the dream. Heather was completely healed and graduated in the top 5 percent of her high-school class. She gave her testimony at the Healing School in Nashville, Tennessee, in February 2005.

Heather had a friend named Monica who also suffered from dyslexia. Heather never told Monica about the vision or what the angels did to her brain. She did, however, declare to Monica, "Jesus is going to heal you!" Heather then prayed for Monica, who fell out in the Spirit. When she got up sometime later, she said that as she lay on the floor, she had a vision of angels coming to her and rewiring her head. Monica was completely healed as well.

Told by Randy Clark in his sermon "Open Heaven"[4]

Ear Missing—Creative Miracle

A young man came for prayer who had one ear on one side of his head and no ear on the other side, not even a hole. I prayed that the Lord would give him a creative miracle. I prayed for the ear that didn't even have a hole, and then I stood ten feet away; and the young man repeated every word I said to him with the other ear plugged.

Tom

Teacher

Global Awakening mission trip to Mexico

---

4 This story can also be found in Guy Chevreau's *Catch the Fire: The Toronto Blessing: An Experience of Renewal and Revival* (HarperCollins, 1994), pgs. 171–74.

Ear Pain

John and I prayed for a little boy about seven years old. His mother said he had pain in his ear for the last two years. Initially, he said he felt a little better but still felt like crying. We asked for more of the Holy Spirit's presence and told him to cry if he wanted. He gently cried and was feeling the presence of God. We finished praying, and he thanked us and seemed to feel a little better. We were praying for his mother when he came running back to tell his mom his ear was all better. He was all smiles! Thank You, Lord!!

John—Pilot
Vicki—Homemaker
Global Awakening mission trip to Mexico

Fibromyalgia; Pain in Knees; Unforgiveness

My cry before leaving Brazil was that I wouldn't go home spiritually dry. For the previous two nights, my dad had held renewal meetings at the beach church where he ministers. Our friends, Zak and Karen-Marie, were the guest speakers and prayer ministers. Zak asked that I help with prayer/prophetic words, so I joined them. Often at the end of the preaching time, God will start pointing people out to Zak, and he will call them forward one at a time and will prophesy over them and record it on tape, then pray for them. So Zak, Karen-Marie (Zak's wife), Candice (an intern from the church), and I were the team. We had prayed for three or four couples when I felt a strong pain in both of my knees. I realized it might be a word of knowledge; and so, when the others were done prophesying, I asked if either of them had knee pain. The wife said she did, that she has suffered from fibromyalgia for two years. As I began to pray, God impressed very strongly upon my mind that I needed to ask her if she had anyone she needed to forgive. She did, and we prayed a prayer of forgiveness. Then, as I began to pray for her knees again, she fell down under the power of God. When she was able to get up, I asked if the pain was gone, and she replied, "Surprisingly, yes it is." Praise Jesus! Later, she sat up and crossed her legs, then looked surprised. "I haven't done that for two years," she said. She gave her testimony that night, and the following night she testified with tears in her eyes that she had gone for a bike ride and kneeled in prayer for the first time in two years. Praise Jesus! Thank You, Lord!

Kathleen
Global Awakening Youth Power Invasion
trip to Curitiba, Brazil

Glaucoma

A seventy-year-old woman asked for prayer for glaucoma in both eyes. I prayed three times for her, asking each time if there was any improvement, and there was. Then the interpreter asked, "Is it perfect yet?" and she replied with tears in her eyes, "Yes! Yes!"

Cindy
Homemaker
Global Awakening mission trip to Colombia

Glass Eye—Creative Miracle; Forgiveness

On the second night, our team went to Bola de Neve Church. They call it the "surfboard church" because the pulpit is a surfboard. At one point, I noticed a man whose eye looked strange. I went over with my translator to ask him what was wrong. He said he had a glass eye because he had been shot in the eye and the doctors could not save the eye. We asked if he wanted prayer, and he did. We prayed for him for about twenty minutes when the Holy Spirit led me to ask him if he still had unforgiveness or bitterness toward the person who shot him. He said yes, he did. We asked him if he wanted to forgive the man, but he did not. Then we explained to him that he must forgive others just as

Jesus forgave us for our sins. He understood. (On this trip, our team had learned that unforgiveness and bitterness are some of the biggest hindrances to healing.) We led him through a prayer to forgive the person, and after maybe ten to fifteen minutes his glass eye turned into a real eye!! It was crazy; both of us were jumping and praising God for what He did. It was a creative miracle!

John
Global Awakening Youth Power Invasion trip to Brazil

Hearing Loss

We were giving words of knowledge when my interpreter, Rodger, stood up. He had hearing loss from playing in a band for many years. Through a word of knowledge, God instantaneously healed his right ear but not the left one. After the ministry team was released to pray for healing, I began to pray for complete restoration of his left ear. It went from 50 percent to 85 percent, and as we continued to pray, one of our team members, Brandon, came over to us. I explained what happened, and Brandon joined in prayer; and the man's hearing was restored 100 percent. I believe the Holy Spirit moved Brandon to pray with us because Brandon is an anointed worship musician. Praise God!

Kaycee, age 16
Global Awakening Youth Power Invasion
trip to Curitiba, Brazil

Hearing Loss; Back Pain

A ninety-eight-year-old woman came to me for prayer. She was deaf in one ear and could barely hear with the other ear, even with her hearing aid. She was also suffering from back pain. I stood behind her and prayed for her back while my interpreter stood in front of her so she could hear him. Then I put my hands over her ears and began to pray for her hearing to be restored. When I removed my hands, she suddenly jerked her head up and began looking around. She reached up and took the hearing aid out and gave us a "thumbs up." When we asked, she said she had about 80 percent restoration of her hearing. We prayed again, and this time she said she had 100 percent hearing. We then asked her about the pain in her back, and she began bending and moving around, then looked up with a big smile and said her back was healed. This woman still makes rugs for a living at ninety-eight years of age, and the pain in her back was making it very difficult for her to work. She almost danced out of the building. Praise God!!

Trish
Global Awakening mission trip to Goiânia, Brazil

Hearing Loss

An older man in his sixties had 50 percent hearing loss after a bad case of the flu. I prayed a couple of short prayers, and he felt tingling and slight improvement. I continued to pray, and each time I checked, his hearing had improved. At one point, he said he heard a roaring noise like a jet engine. As we continued to pray, he heard a pop as his ear opened up. Glory to Jesus!

Jason
Controller
Global Awakening mission trip to Londrina, Brazil

Hearing Loss

During ministry time, one of the young men on the worship team asked for prayer. He was in his twenties and was losing his hearing. Being in my twenties myself and having an emphasis in music, I had an extra measure of compassion for him because I understand how important hearing is for musicians. As I prayed for him, I could see that the Holy Spirit was touching him. I had the interpreter ask if he was feeling anything, and he said there was no improvement in his hearing. I continued to pray, and he started weeping. Crying out to God as if it were my hearing that was impaired, I said, "Heal him! God, please just heal him!" After a time, I wanted to ask what was going on, but my interpreter was deep in prayer with another person so we waited. As I stood there waiting, I thought to myself, "If there is no difference in his hearing, it is going to be really sad, and I do not know what I am going to do." After what seemed like an eternity (but was probably only two minutes), the interpreter asked how he was doing, and he told us his ears were working perfectly! We hugged each other, and when he left to go tell his friends the wonderful miracle God had done, I began to weep. If God had not intervened, this man would have lived in fear of the day when he could no longer hear the music about which he is so passionate. But now he can rejoice and know that when doctors and medical science could not heal him, God did. I too will always remember this and will never be afraid.

Marci
Global Awakening mission trip to Brazil

Labyrinthitis/Balance Issues

I got to pray for a woman with labyrinthitis, which is a condition that affects balance. She was feeling dizzy as she talked to me. I broke the spirit of infirmity off her and soaked her in prayer. All the dizziness and fog left, and her countenance was lighter. Thank You, God!

Wendy
Lawyer
Global Awakening mission trip to Brazil

Meningitis—Deaf-Mute Child

There was a young boy named Alex at one of the services. He was about seven years old. Alex had contracted meningitis when he was three and wasn't able to speak or hear due to complications from the infection.

During the evening service, as people were praying, God touched Alex, and almost immediately he could hear and speak again! God healed him! Thanks be to God, the Lord gave Alex his voice and hearing back. As we were leaving the service that night, I asked him how he was doing, and he shouted praises to the Lord!

Nancy
Homemaker
Global Awakening mission trip to Rio de Janeiro, Brazil

Neck and Leg Pain; Worry

I prayed for a fifty-year-old woman who was suffering from severe pain in her neck and back. The pain also went down her leg all the way to her foot, but it was most severe in her neck and back. She had been suffering from this pain for six months, ever since her husband died. She said she had been worrying about how she would survive without her husband's income. After praying for a few minutes, she indicated nothing was happening. Then the Lord led me to share some Scriptures with her about how He promises to provide for the needs of His people and how we are not to worry about what we shall eat or drink but are to seek Him first and all these other things will be given to us. I then prayed for her again, and I could feel the fire of God in my hands. She said the heat was increasing and the pain was decreasing. I continued praying until her entire body was free of pain. God used His simple truths to set her free.

Richard
Electrician
Global Awakening mission trip to Londrina, Brazil

Paralysis from Automobile Accident; Hip Injury; Salvation

We prayed for a man named Jovan, who was in a wheelchair, paralyzed from the waist down for the last six years due to a car accident that had crushed his third, fourth, and fifth vertebrae. After about ten minutes of prayer, waves of the Spirit's power began surging through his body, and he felt fire in his spine. After another ten to fifteen minutes of these waves of fire we asked him to lift his foot. He moved one foot several inches and then the other! Over the next fifteen minutes, his feet moved more and more to where he was lifting them up nearly twelve inches. Just to make certain, I asked my interpreter to clarify how long it had been since he had moved his foot. Jovan said, "It's been six years. I haven't moved since the accident." We then asked him to lift his knee. He lifted one knee up and then the other! After more prayer, accompanied by wave after wave of the surging power, we asked if he wanted to try to get up and walk. He said he was afraid because his hip was injured as well. We prayed for his hip, and he felt the fire of God in his hip. Then he said he was ready to try to walk. We helped him up and held much of his weight, as his legs were wobbling trying to stand. We sat him back down, and he said excitedly, "I felt the weight on my feet!" He also told us that his hip did not hurt at all. At that point, the team had to leave. We found out that he had received Jesus as his Lord earlier in the service. He said to us, "Jesus has saved my life twice. Once, six years ago, and again today." We spoke to him of the destiny that the Lord has for the rest of his life.

Brent
Pastor
Global Awakening mission trip to Brazil

Paralysis; Weak Ankles

On Sunday morning, I prayed with several Brazilian pastors for a woman who was paralyzed and in a wheelchair. Neither the pastors nor I understood the prayers of each other, but the Holy Spirit understands all languages and empowered our prayers. This woman's legs had no feeling in them. She was in need of surgery and was literally begging on the streets to earn money for the operation. At one point, she came out of the wheelchair and lay on the floor, her legs kicking. I came to understand that one of the Brazilian pastors was praying for feeling in her legs, and after about thirty minutes, she received feeling in her legs! However, as we helped her to stand, we noticed that her feet were turned in and she was standing on the sides of her feet. As I prayed for her ankles to be strengthened, her feet began to straighten out. I actually saw this happen! She then began to walk normally without support! She walked up the steps to the platform with no assistance, then clear across the stage. In her testimony, she said she would no longer need to beg. Glory to God! As the woman returned to her family, the wheelchair was folded up and leaned against the pew. When they went to leave, the woman walked alongside her family, waving farewell! Praise God!

Ellen

Pastor

Global Awakening mission trip to Brazil

Paralysis; Bullet Wound; Forgiveness

Our team was invited to come to the stadium an hour before the service to pray for any sick who wanted to come. Many came, and one after another, most of the people were healed!! As the service began, most of us continued praying for people. At one point, a woman came and took my arm and pulled me to a man in a wheelchair. He had been shot ten months ago in a robbery and had no feeling or movement below his waist. There was no interpreter available, nor was any other team member. I began to pray, accompanied by the fervent prayers of the family. We all prayed for three hours. During that time, the man forgave the person who shot him and repented of falling away from God. He said that when we began to pray, he began to feel heat in his legs. This continued and increased the whole time we were praying. Gradually, movement began to return to his feet. During the time we prayed, we helped him stand three times. Each time, he told us that he could feel more and more of the circulation returning to his legs. He was so happy and said that he hadn't stood since the accident and that it felt so good. They had to leave to catch a bus home, but he left praising God and with great hope for continued healing.

Roberta
Counselor
Global Awakening mission trip to Brazil

Paralysis from Spinal Surgery

A little girl, three years old, was brought to us for prayer. She had been unable to walk since a surgery on her spinal column shortly after birth had left her totally paralyzed. As I looked at her helpless legs, I was filled with Jesus's compassion and His faith because I myself had been born with twisted legs and was unable to walk until God healed me when I was four years old. I prayed briefly, keenly aware that Jesus was doing something beautiful in this little girl's life. After prayer, I honestly didn't see any visible change in her atrophied muscles, but I felt a strong impression to have her stand and try to walk. Her mother stood about ten paces away and called little Jaila to come to her. The little girl falteringly took the first steps of her life. Her mother kept backing up and encouraging her daughter to keep walking. Jaila probably walked for five minutes before we stopped to bless her and thank God for His work. The whole family left ecstatically blessed by what God had done.

Richard
Global Awakening mission trip to Brazil

Right Eye Issues

One night I went with Tom and a group of people from the team to a small church to minister. The church was packed. A lot of people were standing in the back, and kids were sitting on the floor. After praying for many people, I was just sitting on the stage, looking to see if there was anyone else who needed prayer, when a little boy who was maybe ten years old, who had been sitting next to me on the stage, tapped me on the shoulder. There wasn't a translator around, but through gestures I knew he wanted prayer for his eyes, so I began to pray. After a few minutes of prayer, I began to look for a translator so I could ask him questions. A guy from our team offered to translate and found out that the boy had been having problems with his right eye for a long time. They were going to see if glasses would correct the problem, and if glasses didn't work, they were going to have to give an injection in his eye. The translator and I began to pray, stopping a few times to check to see if there was any improvement. As we prayed, his vision improved steadily until it was 100 percent! We asked him to make sure, and he said that he could see the same out of the right eye as his left one! Praise God!! Also, he told us that there was a pain behind the eye, and when we started praying, the pain was the first thing to go.

Alexis, age eighteen
Global Awakening Youth Power Invasion
trip to Curitiba, Brazil

Speech Impediment

Sunday night, a young boy, about eight or nine years old, was brought to us for prayer. His father told us that the boy had a speech impediment. We prayed for him and sensed that God had touched him. Through the translator, we asked the father to see if there was improvement in his son's speech. I went on praying for the next person, and when I looked up, there was the father, crying like a baby. God had healed his son!

Frank
Retail Sales
Global Awakening mission trip to Argentina

Speech Impediment

On Thursday, September 14, 2006, I came to the Methodist church in Washington's Crossing, Pennsylvania, to hear you (Bill Johnson) speak and to witness the miracles that I had only read about in your book and heard about through your sermons on podcast. Not only was I excited to hear you speak and to experience the power of God, but the most pressing issue at the time was our two-year-old daughter. Two weeks earlier, my husband and I had been talking about our daughter Emmy's speech. She had a minor stutter that we were not particularly concerned about because it was infrequent. It typically presented itself when she was excited or trying to pronounce a new word. After we talked, I started to pay close attention to when it happened, and within forty-eight hours the problem had quadrupled! She seemed to be stuttering in everything she said, and it was getting worse—so bad that she began to have facial tics. She would bob her head as she struggled through the beginning sound of each word. She even began to drool and spit when she stuttered. My husband and I were very upset and immediately began fasting and praying. We felt it was an attack from the enemy and were furious that our daughter was the target. We cried out to the Lord together as we never have before in our marriage. Emmy became so frustrated that she stopped talking at times and she stopped singing. Emmy would always sing praise songs in the car or when she would play by herself.

When we found out that the healing conference in Pennsylvania was open to the public, we knew we needed to take her. My sister Jill, Emmy, and I met my mother at the conference. I listened so intently to your sermon, waiting for you to give a testimony of someone healed of a speech problem. I was ready to jump out of my seat and claim that for my daughter, just like the women in your book did. I waited all night for her to receive prayer, all the while being encouraged and blown away by the healings that were taking place before my eyes. Two women next to us who had been healed prayed for Emmy, but as we were packing up to leave, she began stuttering again. I didn't know what to do. Should we just go home and trust that God had begun the healing process? Should we keep praying? Should I take her to the front to be prayed for? I wrestled with this and finally just marched up to the front for prayer, even though you weren't praying for anyone. I kept thinking of the sermon you had preached a couple of years ago about putting yourself in proximity to anointed people. I decided that I wasn't going to leave until Emmy had received prayer in the midst of that kind of anointed power. As I waited behind so many others who wanted to talk to you and Randy, the Lord gave me a vision of the woman who just wanted to touch Jesus's robe and be healed. All I wanted to do was reach out and be in God's presence because I knew He would heal Emmy. After making eye contact with Randy, he listened to my jumbled story as I quickly told him how my daughter had a stuttering problem, and then he pulled you over to pray as well. You both prayed and then asked me to let you know what happened.

Here is the rest of our testimony: Jesus healed Emmy! The stuttering has almost completely stopped, and she is speaking clearly and singing songs to Jesus again! You told me to pray through our house and drive stakes into the four corners of our property, which my husband did the next morning. We have been praying over her every night while she sleeps, and her speech is getting better and better. The first time we noticed it was on Sunday, three days after you prayed for her. I gave a testimony at church of the healing, and then as we sat on the beach that afternoon and watched her play, we just looked at each other amazed. She was not stuttering! Thank You, Jesus! Please share our testimony with others, as I do daily, because I know there is power in our testimony and I expect the Lord to use it to reach others. Thank you for praying for my Emmy. I know it was late and you had had very little sleep, but I am blessed by your willingness to stop and be used by the Lord. Thank you!

Testimony of Jessica as told to Bill Johnson
Washington Crossing Healing School

Spina Bifida

My name is Benjamin. Roughly two years ago, I attended Randy Clark's Healing School with my mother at Christ Community Church in Camp Hill, Pennsylvania. I desired to learn more about the gift of healing and how I could be used by God to minister to the sick. I went with those two intentions alone, even though I had spina bifida since birth and was on crutches and braces for almost twenty-seven years. On the last day of the conference there was a time of impartation prayer. I got in line. Leif Hetland laid hands on me and prayed for me. I was slain in the Spirit and fell to the ground. When I recovered, I got up and got back in line to be prayed for again. Leif smiled and laid hands on me again, and the same thing happened. I fell under the power of the Holy Spirit. This time, as I recovered, I noticed a little eight-year-old girl staring at me. I felt in my spirit that she had something to say to me so I began to talk to her. She was very shy and clinging and whispering to her daddy. Her father told her to tell me what she had told him. She very shyly said, "Jesus told me that this man is going to walk out of this church healed tonight." The adults that were there became excited and dragged me outside the church to see what would happen since the little girl did say I was going to walk out healed. I sat down on the curb and began to talk with them and tell them about my life. I told them that I had always believed that God would heal me, but I also believed God was jealous for the glory, so when it happened, it would not come by the laying on of hands by men. One of the adults there was joking with me and asked me to repeat what I had just said. Pointing to the little girl, he said, "She is not a man; she is a little girl!" At that point, it was like a light bulb went on. All my life, I had looked at the possibility for God to heal me in so many ways, but this was something I had never considered. I became excited.

I could hear praise and worship music coming from the sanctuary, and so I asked the adults if we could go back inside. They told me to go down close to the stairs of the platform leading up to the pulpit. I went to the stairs, sat down, laid aside my crutches, took off my braces, and began to worship. The parents of the little girl gathered all the little children of the church (mostly little girls) who were already walking with the Lord. They gathered around me and began to pray. Some time passed, and they helped me to stand; and we prayed a while longer. Some adults came and wanted to pray as well, but those adults who knew what was taking place asked them to come behind the little ones and pray for their faith to be strengthened, which they did. The children ranged in age from four years old to preteens, and most of them were girls. One of the older girls who was helping lead the prayer asked me if I would try to do something I could not do before. I thought about it and decided to try to raise my hands above my head because my balance had always been so poor that even if I raised my hands just a little, I would lose my balance and fall without my braces or crutches. I told the group of kids that I wanted to raise my hands and asked if they could help me get my hands up. I was suddenly surrounded by many little hands as they all crowded around me and helped me raise my hands. I clapped three times and took a step, and something was different this time. I didn't fall. I began to walk around the church. I walked up and around to the left of the church, up past the sound crew at the doors, to the sanctuary, and back down the other side without falling once. I yelled out, "Praise the Lord!" and was healed. I simply took a step of faith, and the Lord carried me the rest of the way. To God be all the glory!

Benjamin
Camp Hill Healing School

Spina Bifida; Blindness; Intestinal Issues

I prayed for a five-year-old girl named Lena who had spina bifida. She had braces on her legs and could only take two steps with assistance. She had received two hours of prayer with a team member the night before. After about an hour of prayer from me, she started to feel heat in her legs—first at the top, then at the bottom. Then the heat came into her feet, and she said, "I want to walk!" She started walking barefoot and took four steps, and this quickly increased to twelve steps. By the end of the evening, she was jumping up and down!! I also prayed for an elderly blind woman. Within minutes, she received 80 percent of her vision back. She also had a swollen belly from an intestinal problem. We prayed, and her swelling was 25 percent reduced. She will come back tomorrow for more prayer.

Sally
Speech Pathologist
Global Awakening mission trip to Brazil

Spinal Injury; Implanted Metal Issues

I was preaching in my church when a woman ran in and told me I needed to come see what was happening to her fiancé, Charlie. I went out into the hallway, and there was Charlie, shaking because the power of God was all over him. He was going around in circles, making a figure eight. He kept saying, "I don't understand it! I don't understand it!" Finally, I said, "Charlie, what don't you understand?" He went on to explain that seven years ago, he was in a car accident. During surgery, they put steel titanium rods and screws in his back. Since then, he had been in severe pain. He was unable to play with his children and walked hunched over. His body chemistry was causing the screws to dematerialize. He had been to the hospital just the day before, and when the doctor tested for feeling in his legs, he could feel nothing. He had come to church that day dragging his left leg, bent over. Then he told me that while he was worshiping, he saw a ball of fire coming toward him. It hit him, and then the fireball went down his spine and he was instantly healed. The pain was gone!

I was eager for Charlie to give his testimony and invited him to come to the front and share what God had done, but he was scared to speak in front of people. It was his biggest fear. I wouldn't take no for an answer and managed to get him in the sanctuary and up front to tell his story. My wife was so moved that she jumped out of her seat in high heels and a long flowing dress and began to dance before the Lord. That testimony broke our church through to a level of worship we had never before experienced, releasing new levels of joy and celebration in our service.

After his healing, Charlie called me. He was still experiencing the shakes from when the power of God hit him and healed him. God's power would come on him, and he never knew when it was going to happen. When it did, he would start shaking and then run and hide. "How long is it going to last?" he wanted to know. I said, "Listen, Charlie, this is going to be hard for you to understand right now, but I am telling you, enjoy the presence of God because it won't last forever. As long as the power comes, don't be afraid of it. Embrace it, and enjoy it! If you need to go and hide until it passes, that is alright, but enjoy it because it will end at some point."

Randy Clark

A version of this testimony can be found in Randy Clark's
The Thrill of Victory and The Agony of Defeat

Spinal Injury from Surgery; Tumor on Spine

Matilda, the mother of my interpreter (Vanessa), was unable to walk due to complications from surgery to remove a tumor from her spine. She was in a wheelchair. When a word of knowledge was given for a problem in the spine, Matilda felt a wind blow over her. I told Vanessa I would like to pray for her mother. I then shared with Matilda that God had healed me of an incurable disease. I asked her if she believed God could heal her tonight, and she acknowledged that she did. I prayed, asking the Holy Spirit to come and bring healing. When I was done praying, I put my hand out and asked if she wanted to try and walk. She said she did, and so with someone else holding her other hand, she stood, and as she did, strength came into her legs. We were holding her hands, but she was standing on her own. She just cried and cried with joy, and we all praised God together. Then I said to her, "Take a step." She took one step, and then she took another step. She kind of went down a little, but she had strength enough on her own to stand back up and take more steps. I don't know exactly how far she walked—maybe seven feet—but she walked! Glory to the Lord! What an awesome God we serve!

Mary

House Cleaning Business

Global Awakening mission trip to Londrina, Brazil

Tunnel Vision in Left Eye

One day, while at my little Baptist church in Spillertown, Illinois, I was praying for a man with a back problem when all of the sudden I got a sharp pain in my left eye. It is hard to explain, but it felt like something "hit" me twice. The pains only came for a split second each time, and I almost didn't recognize that I was having my first word of knowledge, or at least it was the first time I understood that I was receiving a word of knowledge because I had just recently learned about words of knowledge. I knew I was a Christian with the Holy Spirit living in me and that if I received a word of knowledge, I was obligated to give it. But at the same time that the conviction to give the word rose in me, so did doubt. You see, I had been pastoring this church for seven years, and it had taken me three years to gain the respect of my congregation. The people believed that if you went to seminary, you couldn't have any life in you or any anointing for healing; and I had been to seminary! I thought that if I gave this word of knowledge and it wasn't for anyone, I could lose my congregation's respect. What I had worked hard for three years to gain would be lost in a moment. It was a big risk, but being a man of great faith, I faced that doubt and decided to give the word of knowledge anyway. If nothing else, I would be humbled if I got it wrong. It would be worse not to give the word out of fear and have someone miss their healing. This was the battle that was going on in my mind.

I remember walking up the steps to the pulpit and saying, "I think there might be somebody here who possibly may have something wrong with their left eye." Sister Ruth, who was about six feet two inches tall and about two hundred fifty pounds and who had just buried her husband without shedding a tear, stood to my right. She yelled, "Brother Randy, that's me!" She had tunnel vision in her left eye. I responded, "Well then, come on up here Sister Ruth," and she did. With Sister Ruth standing beside me, I suddenly realized that I didn't know how to pray for the sick. We hadn't gotten that far in the training yet. Feeling like it would be better to have everyone praying for her healing than just me so that we could all share in the defeat if it happened, I called everyone up front. I began to pray for her with the longest prayer that I could imagine. I prayed for the missionaries in Africa, the Sunday school teachers, and everything else that a person could possibly pray for. After I ran out of things to pray for, I finally stopped praying. Sister Ruth said, "Whew, Randy! I'm sure glad you quit praying. I was about to fall on the floor." God totally healed her tunnel vision that day!

Told by Randy Clark in his sermon
titled "Words of Knowledge"

Vision Deterioration; Toe Pain

I prayed for a woman named Vera whose vision had deteriorated to the point where she could no longer read. She was distraught from this handicap. I put my fingers over her eyes and then prayed, allowing the anointing of healing to flow over her. We tested Vera's eyes, and she was able to read a few words from the Bible. Unfortunately, we had to leave shortly thereafter on a bus, so I told Vera to come back to the church and we would finish praying for her eyes. On Sunday, she came again for prayer. I prayed for the ailment to leave her eyes and for the Holy Spirit to heal her in Jesus's name. Afterward, we had her read the Bible, and after a few moments, her voice cracked and tears came to her eyes. She could read! She was healed; praise the Lord! She demonstrated her healing to us a second time by reading music and the Bible. Vera was so moved by her healing that she brought her mother to the evening service for prayer, and God healed the mother from constant pain in her toes.

Neil
Self-Employed
Global Awakening mission trip to Rio de Janeiro, Brazil

REPRODUCTIVE SYSTEM

The REPRODUCTIVE SYSTEM consists of the male and female reproductive organs and glands. Diseases of the reproductive system can be the result of congenital abnormalities, infection, cancers, and environmental factors that cause functional problems.

So God created mankind in his own image, in the image of God He created them; male and female He created them. God blessed them and said to them, "Be fruitful and increase in number; fill the earth and subdue it".
—GENESIS 1:27-28

Breastfeeding Issues

Kaiti had been praying for a woman who had no breast milk. This was the second day she approached us for the same issue. She explained she was a mother of eight children (just like me!) and she was currently nursing almost one-year-old twins. She was exhausted and had no breast milk. The babies were both crying and hungry. We began to pray and prayed for quite a while with no results, just like the day before when Kaiti had prayed. We pressed in, hoping for a miracle. After a while, I heard the Lord say to ask her if she'd had any water to drink. She said only a very little in the morning. Not good for a nursing mom. I nursed seven of mine and know you have to drink a lot of water. We went to get her some and had her drink. Then we went back to praying, and her milk came in and both babies quieted down and nursed happily. We gave her water bottles and told her how important it is that she drink water and eat what she can. It was a practical, life-saving miracle. Thank You, Jesus!!

Tammy—Wife and Mother
Kaiti—Student
Global Awakening mission trip to Mozambique

Breast Pain; Forgiveness

A young mother had to stop nursing her baby because of pain in her breast. I asked if there was any anger toward the baby, her husband, or God, and she said yes, there was. She prayed to forgive them and to change her attitude, and then I prayed for the pain to go away. It seemed to lessen. We prayed again. Later in the evening, she came back and told me all the pain was gone. Thank You, Jesus!

Laurie
Insurance Agent
Global Awakening mission trip to Ukraine

Breast Tumor

A woman came forward for prayer and said that on the previous night, someone had given a word of knowledge about a lump in the left breast. She did not stand up but felt heat in that area, and when she returned home, she found that the lump was smaller. Tonight someone gave the same word, and still she did not come forward. Suddenly, she coughed and tasted blood in her mouth. She spit out the lump and wrapped it in a napkin. She checked her breast, and the lump was gone. She proceeded to tell her story to my translator, Rodrigo, and to show us the lump! I then asked what she needed prayer for. She replied that she had the same problem in her right breast but that the lumps were smaller. We began to pray, and within minutes, she began feeling for the lumps and realized that they were gone as well!

Mary
Global Awakening mission trip to Londrina, Brazil

Endometriosis

Tonight a woman came to us who had had endometriosis for a little over a year. About three months ago, she had surgery for it, and the doctors messed the surgery up. As a result, she had severe, sharp, shooting pain every day. We prayed for a few minutes, and then she went down under the power of God. We asked her if she was feeling anything, but she was not able to speak. We went back to check on her later, and she said that she felt like surgery had been performed while she lay on the floor and the pain was completely gone!

Danielle, age seventeen
Julie, age fifteen
Global Awakening Youth Power Invasion
trip to Curitiba, Brazil

Infertility; Tumor on Back of Head

I am a guitar player who was playing at the Rey De Reyes Church of Pastor Claudio Freidzon in Belgrano, Buenos Aires, when you (Randy Clark) came to speak. During one of the meetings, you gave a word of knowledge, and the presence of God fell very powerfully. My wife had a tumor toward the back of her head that prevented her having a menstrual cycle, so of course we had no children. Beginning that night, the tumor began to dry up and shrink, and three years later we were able to have a precious daughter, even though I was almost forty years old. This is why we love you, pastor Randy, and we always remember you. We even have the video of that service.

Adrian and Gaby
Global Awakening mission trip to Argentina

Ovarian Cyst

One night I had a dream, and the next morning I went over the details in my mind to see if God was trying to tell me something. I didn't get anything specific from the actual plot of the dream but remembered there were two girls named Kelly and Erika in the dream. When it came time for the evening service, I wasn't thinking about the dream anymore. The third person I prayed for was a teenage Brazilian girl who told us through the interpreter that she had a painful cyst on her ovary. As I got ready to pray for her, I asked her name, and she said, "Kelly." I got really excited because I knew God was going to heal her! I told her about the dream to build her faith, and then we all began to pray. After a few minutes of prayer, she said she felt heat. So we prayed a couple minutes more, and she was so filled with the Spirit of God that we had to lay her down. After a few minutes, she got up with no pain! Thank You, Jesus!

Alexis
Global Awakening mission trip to Brazil

RESPIRATORY SYSTEM

The RESPIRATORY SYSTEM consists of the nose and nasal cavity, sinuses, pharynx and nasopharynx, trachea, tracheobronchial system, and the lungs.

Then the Lord God formed a man from the dust of the ground and breathed into his nostrils the breath of life, and the man became a living being.
—GENESIS 2:7

Breathing Issues Since Birth

On this particular day, the team was invited to share words of knowledge. Despite feeling like a novice at this, I shared the impression that God wanted to heal someone who had difficulty breathing. Later, when people were asked to testify of any healings that had taken place, a boy who looked to be about seven or eight years old came and said that he had difficulty breathing, but after the word of knowledge, he could breathe more freely now! When the interviewer asked him how long he had this condition, he said he'd had it ever since he was born! He was very excited and was praising God. My faith was very encouraged. Thank You, Lord!

Wendy
Attorney
Global Awakening mission trip to Brazil

Flu Symptoms—Scratchy Throat, Digestive Upset, Dizziness

I received a word of knowledge about a nineteen-year-old with a scratchy throat. She came forward for prayer, and God healed her and took away the pain in her throat and the gastric issues and dizziness she was experiencing. She told us that all the pain was gone and just a heavy anointing of God remained.

Taylor
Student
Global Awakening mission trip to Brazil

Lung Infection

A little girl named Victoria had an infection in her lungs. The doctors had told the family that they couldn't do anything more for her. I prayed for healing, and about one hour later, the mother, father, and the three children came back onstage and the mother fell on her knees and grabbed me around the legs. She was babbling and crying, and the translator said she was screaming, "Thank you! Thank you!" Victoria had a bowel movement and filled the toilet with infection, and her lungs cleared. The family was praising me and literally kissing me. I said, "Let's praise God—He is the Healer!"

Cookie
Global Awakening mission trip to Manaus, Brazil

Sense of Smell Lost

A man came to me for prayer because he had no sense of smell. I took him over to a side of the church where there was a breeze blowing to see if he could catch the smell of sweetened popcorn coming from outside. When I asked him if he could smell the food, he said that he could not. I prayed for him and then asked him if he could feel anything happening. He was visibly trembling so I knew that he was feeling something. He told me that he could feel the power of God in his body. I asked him if he felt anything going on in the nose area, and he said that the front of his face (basically pointing to the area where the sinuses and nose are) was completely numb. I put my hand back on his face in the "numb" place and prayed some more. Before I could get out more than a few sentences, he opened his eyes and raised his head and began to smile and laugh, saying that he could smell food. My hand that had been on his face was buzzing. He was healed! Then he asked me if I could pray for him to be filled with the Spirit. I put that same hand on him, and he doubled over in a heap on the ground and began to tremble under the power of God. He was probably around twenty-five years old.

Ben, age twenty-three
Global Awakening Youth Power Invasion
trip to Curitiba, Brazil

Sinus Condition

I prayed for a young woman who had suffered from a sinus condition for many months. I had only been praying for a few minutes when she began to feel heat. I continued to pray for her, and the power of God came over her and she fell out in the Spirit. She lay on the floor and shook violently in the anointing of the Lord. I continued to pray for others as God worked in her. After several minutes, she got up, and I asked what happened. She was completely healed and had experienced the fire of God all over her body! There was such an open Heaven here tonight!

Cathy

Project Manager

Global Awakening mission trip to Brazil

Sleep Apnea

My name is John. I'm a member of Pastor Rodney Hogue's church, Community of Grace, in Hayward, California. Pastor Hogue referred me to you the last day of the Leaders Advance meeting at Bethel Church. This is the testimony of how my son, John Paul, was healed of clinical sleep apnea during the Youth Power Invasion mission trip to Brazil in 2005. I'll try to be brief as possible. John Paul was diagnosed with clinical sleep apnea in late 2001 by Kaiser Permanente in Hayward, California. In September 2001, he underwent surgery to remove his tonsils and adenoids in the hope that this procedure would clear up his sleep apnea. A head and neck surgeon performed the surgery. Post-surgery sleep studies revealed that John Paul still had clinical sleep apnea and needed to start using a CPAP machine. From October 2001 to July 2005, John Paul had to use the CPAP machine every night while he slept. He even took the machine to the Global Awakening Youth Power Invasion mission trip in the summer of 2005. I'll let John Paul describe what happened in his own words. The following is taken from the testimonial letter he sent out to those who sponsored him on the trip:

> Hey everybody. It's JP. I'm back from Brazil, and I'm writing some of my testimonies down so you can hear what happened down there. Some healing happened to me while I was down there. I had a sleep disorder called sleep apnea. My airway would close during my sleep, not letting me breathe without a CPAP machine. Randy Clark gave a word of knowledge about someone who has a disease that doesn't let them breath while they're asleep. The Holy Spirit came into my throat. I felt the Holy Fire. I was inhaling air for about two minutes. I thought I was going to pass out. God told me He healed me so I believe God healed me during the trip. After I returned home, my parents had Kaiser Permanente run an overnight sleep study just to make sure. I am blessed to report that on 8/3/2005, my mom got the results of the test. Praise God, the test proved I was healed! The oxygen content was normal, whereas before, a similar test detected my sleep apnea.

The physician's letter said, "The results are not consistent with clinical sleep apnea." My wife, who is also a RN at Kaiser, took the results to the surgeon who did the original surgery on John Paul. She used the results to witness to the doctor, who noted that we had a real miracle on our hands. Subsequently, the healing testimony has taken on a life of its own. A teacher friend of my wife in the Philippines took John Paul's testimony and put it in the local high-school newspaper and was subsequently contacted by many people who read about the miracle, some believing God for their own healing. During a trip to the Philippines in March 2006, others sick with cancer, renal failure, etc., wanted John Paul to pray for them. All this happened because Randy Clark is faithful to the call of God on his life. If it weren't for the Lord Jesus Christ using Global Awakening, John Paul could have missed his healing. Greater still, the increase of God's call on John's life wouldn't be what it is today if it weren't for the ministry opportunities afforded by Global Awakening. John Paul will be going back to Brazil this summer. Please pass on our extreme gratitude to all those who made John Paul's healing possible.

John

Tuberculosis; Fear; Forgiveness

At the beginning of the preaching, the youth pastor's wife asked if I could leave the service to go pray for a young lady diagnosed with tuberculosis. She was spitting up blood through her nose and was too weak to remain at the meeting. Three of us went and prayed for her. There appeared to be no results from our praying. God revealed that the young lady had fear and unforgiveness. After working through these, another pastor came and asked me to anoint her with oil. She began to feel heat on her back. Then we noticed that the rattle in her breathing was gone. We continued praying, praising God and focusing on Jesus, the Healer. Her father came to take her home, and I felt we needed to continue praying a bit longer. I hugged the father, and he shook and was slain in the Spirit. The young lady ended up feeling 100 percent well and had to wait for her father to get up from the floor so they could leave!

Judy
Missionary
Global Awakening mission trip to Brazil

Vocal Cords Damaged

I gave my first word of knowledge on the platform with Randy and the team during a mission trip to Brazil. Immediately, I could see at least four hands raised and waving to indicate a response to the word, and then as an indication of instant healing. My personal favorite was a young lady in her twenties who had lost her singing voice to an illness two years prior. It took some perseverance in prayer, but in the end, she and I sang a duet together, she in Portuguese and me in tongues.

Paul
Global Awakening mission trip to Brazil

Vocal Cords Damaged

An older man came for prayer. He looked to be about sixty and of modest means, though not poor. My translator had difficulty understanding his request, but he did hear him say, "I have no words." An accident of some kind years ago had damaged his upper body and his neck and vocal cords, and he was only able to say a couple of words to us. He couldn't speak in sentences or have normal conversations. Christian (the pastor's son) and I prayed over him and placed hands on his neck area. After ministering like this for a while, Christian checked again, and I could hear the man repeating some words over and over with more clarity and volume. "What did he say?" I asked. Christian replied, "He says, 'I got words! I got words! I can talk! I am talking,'" over and over. He was very happy. Praise God for whom all things are possible!!

William
Global Awakening mission trip to Colombia

SKELETAL SYSTEM

The SKELETAL SYSTEM consists of the bones, cartilage, joints, spine, vertebrae, and skull. It is the framework of the body and contains two hundred and six bones, including six very small bones in the middle ear (three per ear). The muscles of the body attach to the bones, allowing for the movement of the joints. All told, the skeletal system supports the body, allows for movement, offers protection, produces new blood cells, and stores calcium.

Strengthen the feeble hands, steady the knees that give way; say to those with fearful hearts, "Be strong, do not fear; your God will come...."
—ISAIAH 35:3-4

Arthritis in Feet

A woman, about forty-five years old, presented herself for prayer for arthritic pain in her feet. She was very overweight and had suffered greatly from excruciating pain for a very long time. We prayed for a while with no visible effect. Then I asked, "Lord, what should I do?" He said, "Anoint her feet with oil, and pray again." I had her sit on the altar steps and remove her shoes. I then poured oil on my hands and massaged her feet, anointing them. Then I prayed again. This time all pain left her feet. By His stripes she was healed! Glory to God! Praise the name of Jesus!

Rob
Global Awakening mission trip to New Zealand

Back Pain; Dislocated Spine

It was our last night in Volta Redonda, Brazil. After the impartation prayer segment, I turned around to pray for someone. There was a man I had seen earlier going through the fire tunnel. He had been stumbling along using forearm brace crutches. He was around three hundred and fifty pounds and obviously in a lot of pain with every step he took. I asked the Holy Spirit to come, and the man went down in the Spirit rather quickly. I kept praying over his legs. An interpreter was brought over. I asked the man if he could stand. He did, and I started walking with him; and he just winced in pain and needed to sit. We interviewed him and found that he had a dislocated back and was going in for surgery in two weeks, but he could not afford the surgery. As he was sitting in the chair, I placed my hand on the area of his back and started praying, asking the Holy Spirit and healing angels to bring healing. After a little while, I asked if he was feeling anything, and he said that his back was cracking and popping and fire was going up and down his left leg. "More, Lord. Bring complete healing in Jesus's name," I said. A few

233

moments went by, and I asked him to stand and walk a little bit. I took him by the hands. He took a couple of hesitating "stiff-legged" steps, and then he let go of my hands and started walking normally on his own. I then asked him if he could bend forward. He not only bent forward, he bent side to side and front to back with a huge smile on his face. I asked where his wife went, and he pointed at a woman with her mouth open watching him walk freely. We both started jumping up and down thanking Jesus. You are so good!!!

Ed
Sleep Technologist
Global Awakening mission trip to Brazil

Back Pain

I was in a hospital in southern Illinois in a coal-mining community, praying for a guy, when I heard moaning across the hallway. I went across the hall and knocked on the door, and a woman invited me in.

"Hi! My name is Randy Clark, and I'm a Baptist pastor," I said. "I heard you moaning in pain, and I believe that God can heal; and I want to pray for you. Can I pray for you?"

"No! You can't," she said.

"Well, why not?" I replied.

"Because I don't believe that it would do any good," was the reply.

"Well," I said, "you may be right, and probably are, but you don't have anything to lose."

She said she was a coal miner and the roof had caved in on her and amputated her leg. She had also suffered an injury to her spine and was in severe pain. Then she told me that she had been to Tulsa to a camp meeting of Kenneth Hagin's. She went believing that if Hagin prayed for her, she would be healed. Hagin did indeed pray for her, but she wasn't healed. She thought that if Hagin's prayers hadn't healed her, mine certainly wouldn't.

There are anointed people, and Kenneth Hagin was one of them. He was an anointed man of God with a powerful ministry for healing, and I honor him. This testimony is not meant in any way to disparage his name. He heard from the Lord and was very intimate with the Lord. That being said, I still believed that she had nothing to lose by having me pray for her. We talked a little more, and she finally agreed to let me pray. I prayed for her, and her headaches and severe pain left. This shocked her and me because there was hardly any faith for healing in the room, and I wasn't the anointed person. In fact, this was one of the first healings I ever saw in my life. This experience illustrated to me that everybody can be used for healing in Jesus's name. If I had turned the principle of "must be anointed for healing to pray for healing" into a law, I would not have prayed for her and she might not have been healed. God can use anyone, even little ol' me and you. You don't have to be the anointed person of God to pray for the sick. It is my experience that more people get healed when more people pray for healing.

Told by Randy Clark in *The Thrill of Victory and The Agony of Defeat*

Back Pain

Sebastian, a young man of about seventeen, wanted me to pray for his back. He was in quite a bit of pain and was unable to bend or lift anything. I prayed, and he went down in the Spirit. When he got up, he was 100 percent healed. He said that he felt a crunch as he went down. The Lord must have been putting his spine into alignment. The next day, he was still 100 percent pain-free and was smiling from ear to ear. This was my very first instant healing in fifteen years of praying for the sick!! God is so good.

Pat

Retired

Global Awakening mission trip to Argentina

Back Realignment

A university professor named Maria was invited to the evening meeting by her coworker and my interpreter, Suzanna. During worship, she asked Suzanna why people raised their hands during worship. Suzanna asked me, and I explained that it was an expression of praise to God. Maria came up for prayer and asked if I would pray for healing in her back. Maria had much pain across the top of her back so I invited the Holy Spirit to come with His healing presence. As we waited on the Lord, I asked her if she had invited Jesus Christ to be her Lord and Savior. She replied, "So-so" and that she was a Catholic and sometimes she believed and other times she did not. She said she was very "rational," which I presumed meant that she had some intellectual hang-ups with the Gospel. I explained that the Gospel of Jesus Christ was a simple message and that God was not after our mind as much as He was after our heart. I explained that the Gospel was so simple that even children can understand it. As we were dialoguing over these things, I heard a popping noise, like joints snapping. I looked at her back, and the bones and muscles in her upper back were moving and snapping back and forth across her back. It was very audible and visible. I looked over at Suzanna a few feet away, and she had turned to see what the noise was. We were both amazed. I didn't know for sure if it was God or powers of darkness. I quietly declared that all powers of darkness must submit to the authority of Christ. But her muscles and vertebrae continued to move and crack. It looked like an angel was giving her back a chiropractic adjustment. I tried to ignore it and continued to show the reality of God's love for her. She was a little unsettled with all the commotion going on in her back but was intent on hearing what I said. She responded by saying that the words that I spoke were sinking deep into her heart, and then she asked, "What's happening to my back?" I said, "I think you're getting an adjustment by God." I asked her how it felt, and she began moving her shoulders and arms around and exclaimed that her back was healed. It was amazing! She left with a smile on her face, and I believe she now has a reason to believe the Gospel. She said she would consider all these things.

Dennis
Pastor
Global Awakening mission trip to Brazil

Back Realignment

An older lady came for prayer. She had several back injuries that kept her in much pain. She had spent a lot of money on drugs and electric shock treatment, trying to control the pain, with no relief. After praying, she got up off the floor pain-free and was very happy! She said she felt the bones in her back being moved around, starting at the top of her back and moving all the way down, as if someone was moving them into place!

Jean
Writer
Global Awakening mission trip to Brazil

Bone Spur on Right Hip

During the lunchtime ministry session, Rachel, Jennifer, and I laid hands on a woman with some kind of bump (or bone spur) on her right hip that had been causing a great deal of pain and hindering movement. As we waited on the Holy Spirit for direction, I recalled how God had been dealing with me in particular about not overcomplicating things and about how healing has nothing to do with what you do or how you do it; it has everything to do with obedience to the Holy Spirit and faith that He's with you. As we waited, I heard a simple command along the lines of, "In the name of Jesus Christ, bump, disintegrate!" I spoke the command, but nothing visible or tangible took place; and she felt nothing. We asked her to test and see if the pain was gone. She stood up and began to move around and told us that she could still feel the lump and certain movements were still painful. Rather than getting wrapped up in whether or not I had missed God or didn't hear the Holy Spirit correctly, we sat her back down and waited on the Holy Spirit again. Again, I felt the Holy Spirit prompting me to command basically the same thing a second time. I chose not to get rational about it but just to obey the prompting. I am not sure how the second command was different or even if it was different. But this time, though she didn't feel anything, when she got up to test it out, the bump was miraculously gone and she had full movement and no pain! She was doing all kinds of deep squats and lunges and hip rotation movements with great excitement on her face. We exalted and lifted up the wonderful name of Jesus together, and then we laid hands on her and commanded some kind of "skin thing" to be clear in Jesus's name. We all knew by faith that it was done. Though we didn't see any visible change, no one felt any need to do anything further; God was with us, and we walk by faith and not by sight!! To Him be all the glory!

James
Personal Trainer
Global Awakening mission trip to China

Calf and Ankle Injury

On Friday night, I prayed for a man whose calf and ankle had been terribly injured in a car accident. The calf and ankle were swollen to twice the size of the other leg, and he had very little mobility. As I prayed, he felt electricity shooting through his leg. He began to have muscle spasms. The swelling in his leg immediately disappeared, and the motion in his foot and ankle were restored!

Dave and Anita
Global Awakening mission trip to Colombia

Feet—Pain and Multiple Surgeries

I prayed for a lady who had suffered with pain in her feet for a few years. She had been to the doctor and had multiple surgeries, but her feet were worse than ever. She reported that she felt 80 percent better when I started to pray for her. I asked the Holy Spirit to come and touch her feet and cast out the pain in the name of Jesus. She reported that her feet were tingling, so I knew God was touching her. I kept praying. When I asked again about the pain in her feet, she said it was getting worse. After casting out the pain and the spirit of infirmity, I again asked for the Holy Spirit to come and heal her feet. When I asked about the pain again, she said it was gone. This was the first time that I laid my hands on someone and saw God heal them on the spot.

Beth, age eighteen
Global Awakening Youth Power Invasion
trip to Curitiba, Brazil

Foot—Broken

My wife and I saw a woman who had a plastic removable cast on her foot and felt the Lord leading us to pray for her foot to be healed. We laid our hands on her foot and asked the Lord to heal her, and in minutes the pain was gone. She took off her cast and was able to walk on the foot. We finally asked her what was wrong with her foot, and she said she had broken it eight days ago!

Barry and Lynn
Global Awakening mission trip to Vitória, Brazil

Foot—Broken

There were about fourteen of us in intersession, worshiping in the Spirit. I felt the Holy Spirit lead me to impart to those in intercession. The anointing was powerful. I went to anoint Victor first. When I laid my hands on him, the power of God hit him like lightning. He flew into the air, and as he fell out into the Spirit, one of his feet came down on my bare right foot. His heel tore and crushed my foot. I knew I was hurt, but I continued to pray for the rest of the team. I stayed in the Spirit and felt great love and power. The Father had me pray and impart anointing and then release a prophetic psalm. Then I started to prophesy these lines: "I come to the mountain of fire, falling at feet pierced with resurrection glory. My heart yearns; my flesh submits. Both give way for my spirit to soar to the heights of glory found at resurrected feet." The pain in my foot was intense by this time. It was throbbing and bleeding. I came to a place in the Spirit where I thanked God for allowing me to be a prophetic sign in the fellowship of His suffering. Jim and Carter came over to pray for me. I had great grace to stay in the Spirit and lead intercession while they prayed for my healing. The pain made me nauseated. They prayed for the pain and nausea to leave, and it did. They said the wound was deep and the bone was broken and that swelling and bruising had started. They said it was very serious—they could see the bone. As they prayed, Valerie and Rafa joined them. They prayed for knitting together and mending and then watched as the bone healed, the wound closed, the swelling went down. They prayed for about two hours while I was in the Spirit facilitating intercession from the heavenly realms. Angels came, releasing God's love and light. My foot was completely healed except for a very small flesh wound, which I believe was a reminder of what God had done. I have a holy scar as testimony of God's supernatural healing. Praise God for His beautiful Church, who stayed with me and prayed me through to healing. I see their faithfulness as a prophetic sign of the Body of Christ being healed and knit together.

Tracee

Global Awakening mission trip to Brazil

Fingers—Broken and Improperly Set; Forgiveness

A young man requested prayer for crooked fingers that resulted from being broken and improperly set. The middle joint of the finger was enlarged and painful. As we started the prayer, I asked him if he could forgive the medical people for the improper set. Immediately, he did. After a short time of prayer, he indicated that he felt heat in the finger. I prayed for the pain to go, checking periodically for movement and pain level. After a short time, he said the pain was gone. I dealt with a spirit of arthritis in the joints, with continued checks for range of motion. At one point, I asked him to look at the finger. He said that the joint looked smaller, which confirmed my observation. I suggested that he continue daily prayer for his finger and to exercise the joints. I suggested ways to counter the lies of the enemy if he began to think nothing had changed. I prayed blessings over him and asked God for a completed work. During the Sunday service, I found the man, and he told me that he no longer had pain in the finger. Praise God for His love and healing work!

Art
Retired
Global Awakening mission trip to Spain,
England, and Switzerland

Head Injury—Lump on Forehead

It's hard to put this trip into words. I saw God move in so many different ways. One way was through physical healings. I saw many healed from knee, back, stomach, and head problems. One of my favorite healings was when I prayed for a child who had a bump sticking out of his forehead. His mom said it happened when he was jumping and playing. I began to pray and couldn't really see a difference at first, but after about twenty minutes or so, I took a look and the bump was barely visible. I would have prayed more, but it was time to leave. God is good!

Although I saw a lot of miracles, they are nothing compared to what God has been teaching me. He's been stripping and breaking me and showing me more of what love really looks like—how selfless it really is and that you can give love in so many different ways, by serving people. There's still so much I'm trying to take in, but I know that I'll be taking back so much from this trip that is going to impact me for years to come.

Sandrine
Student
Global Awakening mission trip to Mozambique

Head Injury; Headache

I prayed for a woman who had suffered from a headache every day and night for the past two years. Through the interpreter, I found out that she had hit her head on a building two years ago and that was when the headaches began. When I started praying for her, she began to cry. I asked the Lord to lift the trauma of the injury from her, comfort her, and heal her by His Spirit. In a short time, she said the pain was completely gone. She was smiling and happy—pain-free for the first time in two years! Thank You, Lord!

Wendy
Lawyer
Global Awakening mission trip to India

Head Injury; Pain; Knee Pain

On Monday morning, a woman came for prayer. She had injured the back of her head in a bus accident over twenty years ago and had been in severe pain ever since. I started praying for her, asking her to forgive the bus driver for causing her injury, and prayed the command prayer,

"Be healed in the name of Jesus." I kept asking the Holy Spirit to come with His healing power. The Lord healed her pain 100 percent, and she was weeping with joy that the severe pain had finally gone! She had also slipped a few days earlier and hurt her knee. I prayed the command prayer once again, with my hand on her knee, and once again 100 percent of the pain went away after a few minutes of calling on the Holy Spirit. She was ecstatic and kept hugging me and the interpreter while shouting out praises to God.

Rose

Homemaker

Global Awakening mission trip to Rio de Janeiro, Brazil

Hip Pain

After lunch, several of our group went for a walk through town. As we approached the stores, I told one of my companions that I had a word of knowledge of pain in the left hip. A woman came out of one of the stores, and recognizing us as Americans who were at the Global Awakening conference, she wanted to know more. She then began to tell us about the pain she was having in her left hip! She said she would come to the healing service tonight. We asked if we could pray right then, and she agreed. I placed my hand on the pain, and the other team members entered in; and she was healed right then. God is good! Later, we heard stories of her testimony from others on the street as she told them about her healing.

Don

Home Builder

Global Awakening mission trip to Brazil

Hip—Smashed Hip Bone; Salvation

Randy called out a word of knowledge for hips. A man on crutches responded. He was scheduled for surgery the following day. He had fallen and smashed his hipbone. The surgeon had placed a pin in his hip, and he had been in pain for two years. I asked him if he had accepted Christ. He said no, this was his first time at the church. I led him to Christ, and he said as soon as he accepted Jesus as his Savior, the pain left. I asked him if he would like to give me his crutch and walk. He reluctantly gave it to me, took a step, and then walked across the stage! Glory to God!

Tom Hauser

Global Awakening mission trip to Manaus, Brazil

Knees; High Blood Pressure; Leg Length Discrepancy; Hip and Spinal Alignment

I was asked to pray for an elderly lady with two bad knees. Her left knee needed an operation, but her doctor was waiting for her blood pressure to stabilize. He had put her on new medication that was making her sick. I also found out later that her left foot turned inward and her right leg was shorter than the left. I prayed for healing in both her knees, for her blood pressure, for the tendons in her ankle to strengthen, for her foot and leg to lengthen, for her hip to be healed, for her back and spine and hips to align themselves, for her muscles to strengthen, and for her body to straighten. Afterward, she was able to sit down easier, could flex her knees, could rotate her ankle easily, her legs looked the same length, and she was able to walk around the front of the church without any assistance. She walked out of the sanctuary carrying her cane!

Taraden

Global Awakening mission trip to Australia

Knee—Dry Socket

During one of the meetings, I prayed for a woman who had a dry socket in her knee. Her leg was very swollen. As I began to pray, she started to giggle, and the interpreter started to giggle too. Under my hand I could feel movement under the skin. I prayed that the Lord would put squishy stuff between the joints. She said her knee got real warm and she could feel liquid deposited in between her kneecap and joint. I blessed what the Lord was doing, and the Lord continued to touch her for quite some time.

Lisa
Church Janitorial Staff
Global Awakening mission trip to Brazil

Knee—Surgically Implanted Material

A man came for prayer for his knee. He had been in a motorcycle accident and had had six surgeries on his right knee. The surgeon had inserted a metal bar that was fifteen centimeters long from his hip down. He couldn't bend his knee, much less bring his weight back up. We prayed for him and then asked him to try to stand and do what he hadn't been able to do. He stood up and was able to bend, and he lifted the other leg and came back up with one leg.

Attendee
Global Awakening mission trip to Brazil

Knees—Turned-Out Kneecaps; Pain; Lameness

A ten-year-old boy who could not fully walk, run, or jump since he was one year old was brought up for prayer. His kneecaps were turned out, but the doctor did not know the cause. After walking a few steps, he would fall over. We prayed by laying hands on his knees, and the pain diminished. We prayed again, and he felt an unfamiliar pain pulling one of the kneecaps back to center. We prayed again, and all the pain was gone. He was able to walk and run and jump without issue and with a big smile on his face. Thank You, precious Lord!

Kathleen
Pastor
Global Awakening mission trip to Brazil

Leg—Broken Tibia

Twenty-four-year-old Julia walked into Saturday night's healing meeting on crutches and left celebrating the healing of a broken leg. She had broken the tibia bone in her leg three weeks earlier while training with too much intensity for a marathon. When the prayer time began, Julia said she felt the peace, love, and mercy of God envelop her. "I felt peace about many things," she said. She was healed without anyone laying a hand on her and left the building holding her crutches high. The next day, she was able to take a long walk without pain, and she returned for the Sunday meeting without crutches. We even took a photo of her after her healing.

Barbara
Antique Dealer
Global Awakening mission trip

Leg—Broken; Femur Bone

A woman named Anna asked for prayer. She had fallen and broken her leg, driving the femur bone out of place. She was in a cast from her knee to her foot. Her toes were exposed. As two of us prayed for her, I put my hands around her ankle area. My prayer partner felt the hole by her knee where the bone was supposed to be. My hands became hot and so did her cast. I asked my partner to see if he felt the heat, and he did. I moved my hands halfway up the cast and checked to see what was happening. Anna was feeling the heat too. We continued to pray and then interviewed her again. She responded by saying, "Hot" and "No more hole." It appeared her bone had moved back into place, but she still had pain in her foot so we prayed again and the pain left completely. We found out later that she has a doctor's appointment scheduled to verify her healing.

Joyce
Homemaker
Global Awakening mission trip to Vitória, Brazil

Leg and Arm Length Discrepancy

A girl from our team called me over to help her pray. She was praying for a guy whose right arm and leg were shorter than the left. At the start of the prayer, I had all the faith in the world. As I prayed, his arm began to grow. And it wasn't like it grew a little bit—it grew an inch or so. Then I started on the legs. Again, God showed up, and his leg grew. I asked him to check things out—to walk around a little. When he did, we could see that he was walking straight, which he hadn't been able to do since he had been in an accident when he was eight. God healed him!

James, age fifteen
Global Awakening Youth Power Invasion
trip to Curitiba, Brazil

Leg Length Discrepancy; Back Pain

During one of the services, I noticed a little boy about four years old. He was sitting on a woman's lap. His aunt told me that he had one leg that was much shorter than the other. The difference appeared to be as much as two inches. She told me that when he was six months old, his mother abused him and broke the femur bone in his leg. This was the reason for the difference in length. Then the boy was put into an institution for three years as an orphan. This past year, a couple adopted him, and they drove about four hundred miles to come to our meeting. I held his legs out together and began to pray. To my amazement, after only several minutes, I began to notice that the short leg seemed to be getting longer. As I commented on this, it suddenly matched the other leg in length perfectly. We all began rejoicing at the glorious work of the Lord right before our eyes. The woman then put the boy down on the floor to walk as she and his father watched. He walked with no limp. We were all very excited and captured the moment on video. Two days later, I was in the intercessory prayer room during the service. We were told that two pastors were coming in for prayer. One of the men was the boy's father. As we prayed over them, many felt that these two men were significant to revival in Brazil. The boy's mother and father told me that he no longer had back pain and that he is walking perfectly now. They laughed as they told me that he runs so much now it is difficult for them to keep up. I so loved watching the Lord touch this little one who used to be an orphan. This is the Father's heart!

Patty
Homemaker
Global Awakening mission trip to Curitiba, Brazil

Leg Length Discrepancy; Back Pain

During the ministry time, after Tom preached, a woman with back pain—mostly at the base of her neck, but all over her upper and lower back as well—approached me for healing. After laying hands on her and commanding her to be healed, her back got very hot, and she was instantly relieved of most of her pain. The Holy Spirit spoke to me that she had a short leg or something out of alignment in her neck, back, or hips that caused one leg to appear shorter. So, I sat her down on a stool against the wall. I made sure that she sat up very straight with her back all the way against the wall, and then I checked her legs. Sure enough, her right leg was a half-inch shorter than the left. By this time, three other Chinese women had gathered around us. Up to this point, I had been communicating only through hand signals and charade—like acting. I was going to command the short leg to line up—something I've done many times before—with faith that it would easily be done again. But the Holy Spirit had the great idea to actually have them pray for her healing. So I grabbed Leah, a translator, and a little crowd gathered around us. I asked, "Who wants to command the leg to line up and perform a miracle in Jesus's name?" One Chinese sister eagerly jumped at the opportunity so I showed her how to hold the feet so she and the onlookers could all see the realignment take place and the heels become perfectly even. Then I told her to command the spine and hips to realign in Jesus's name and to do anything else the Holy Spirit might show her to do or say. I held my finger across the heel of her left (longer) leg and stuck it straight out across the short heel, revealing the half-inch gap. Then the woman began to command, and we all watched as the short leg grew out until the right heel touched my extended finger—perfectly even with the left. Not only did all those people learn how to work with the Holy Spirit, but one of them actually got to do it; and they all witnessed a miracle. And on top of all that, the woman who was sitting on the stool in need of a miracle got up totally realigned and pain-free! Jesus received praise, honor, and glory and continues to do so!

James
Personal Trainer
Global Awakening mission trip to China

Leg Length Discrepancy; Crooked Leg

On Thursday night, Randy began to minister to the sick. Several team members came forward with words of knowledge, and people were responding by standing up. My attention was drawn to one of those standing—a man in his late thirties. He had responded to a word of knowledge but did not appear to be experiencing God's touch at all. It seemed like a good thing to go over and pray for him. I began to interact with him and his wife, who was translating for us, as he knew very little English and I knew very little Portuguese. I came to understand that he had some sort of problem with his left leg and had had multiple surgeries, but the doctors had told him it would get worse and worse—that there was nothing more they could do for him. The left leg had grown longer than the right, and the difference in the two could be expected to get worse. I didn't really know what to do. I checked first for any occult involvement, but there appeared to be none. He came from a Christian background and also had gone through spiritual housecleaning for any alliances made by past generations. So I just prayed. We broke the power of the doctor's bad report. What I felt impressed to tell him was that over the next few days, the Lord would heal him, and that the healing even of the scars from surgery would confirm that it was done. With great trepidation, I shared this with them. He and his wife were very excited and grateful for the prayers. I didn't know if I was acting on great faith or if I was a chicken for not going for it right then.

His wife came up later and asked me if that word really was from the Lord. I told her honestly that I felt that it was what God had put on my heart but that I may have heard incorrectly. I told her that I wanted to be responsible for my words and asked them to come to me within two days and tell me whether or not the words I had spoken came to pass. Before this trip I had never pursued physical healing, although I was quite comfortable with inner healing-type prayer. I prayed for this man a lot that night and the next morning. Maybe I was also praying for myself—I felt I had really gone out on a limb. The next morning after the service ended, his wife came to me to ask for more prayer for him. I began to pray, and she began to interpret. I now began to understand his situation further, and we determined that even though his left leg had grown too fast, it seemed like God is more into growth than the reverse, so we prayed for his right leg to grow out to match his left. I had more faith that day because my wife, Pam, had just seen a leg grow out when she prayed the night before, and she had shared the story with me. I saw her and called her over. She came over and had him sit down and proceeded to hold his legs in her hands as we prayed. Then we all saw it—the wife, Pam, and myself: right before our eyes, the leg quickly grew out two centimeters (an inch) to match the other one. It was the funniest thing I have ever seen. I started laughing. His wife started crying. We all started praising God. The man then pointed out that the left one had grown curved, and so Pam put her hands on each side of it and commanded it to straighten. We all rejoiced, and then Pam and I had to pray for others. Talking to the couple later, we found that this condition had plagued him all of his life. He couldn't join with the others at school because of this disability, and he was mocked and teased for it. His disappointment had led him to grow cold in the things of the Lord. But God had mercy on us all. Oh, and the left leg—it is now straight as well. Maybe I didn't get the word completely right the first night, but God blessed us all with a mighty move that none of us will ever forget.

My wife saw this couple again about a year later. He was still doing fine and was very grateful to God. The growth abnormalities that had overgrown and twisted his leg had stopped. And they now had a one-year-old daughter named Vitória (Victory), and he can run and play with her.

Don
Global Awakening mission trip to Londrina, Brazil

Leg—Surgically Implanted Material

A woman came to the meeting seeking prayer for her legs. Seven years ago, she had been in an accident and broken many bones. She had a metal bar in her leg with eight screws. There was a huge screw in her knee. She also had two bars and two pins in her other leg. She'd had five surgeries in all. She couldn't bend her knees or cross her legs. Her son begged her to come to the meetings. During the teachings she began to feel faith for her healings. We prayed for her, and she felt heat. When she tried to move her hips and legs, all of her movement was restored!

Global Awakening mission trip to Londrina, Brazil

Neck Injury; Pain; Migraine-Like Headaches

This is the testimony of Randy Ostrander as told by Randy Clark: I was in Melbourne, Florida, conducting a revival. There was a pastor there named Randy Ostrander who had started a church in Melbourne,

Florida, that had grown in a few years to an average attendance of six hundred. He was an athlete and held a high hurdles record. He had also been a pro football draft choice and was known locally for his athletic abilities. One day, he was working out, pushing weights, when the machine broke and the weights fell down across his neck, doing severe damage. He had to have three vertebrae fused during different surgeries and had been in uncontrollable pain since the surgeries despite taking the highest dosage of pain medication possible. He had been this way for six years when I met him. For six years, he could not be around loud noise of any kind due to the terrible migraine-like headaches he suffered every waking moment of his life since the accident. He was totally disabled, unable to play with his kids or pastor his church.

He was a Word of Faith pastor and had established a faith school of healing in his church. After the accident, he went to some of the most famous healing people in that movement to be prayed for, but he hadn't been healed. He had been prayed for over a hundred times and hadn't been healed. He came to the meeting in Melbourne and stood in faith for healing. I prayed for him, and absolutely nothing happened. The next day, he set up a meeting with his wife and me and shared the whole story. As I share this testimony, I want you to understand that lots of people come to me and don't get healed. I know this happens to others who pray for healing as well. This is just a reality we live with. Everybody has people they pray for who don't get healed. If you are someone who has not been healed after much prayer, don't be discouraged. Just because someone prays for you and you don't get healed that particular time doesn't mean you are not going to get healed. I don't know why; I don't have an answer for it. Just keep pressing in for you healing.

As Randy and his wife shared more details of their story, his discouragement was evident. He was on high dosages of medication, but nothing was working so he had started taking his medicine with whiskey to try to cut the pain. He felt he couldn't go on. At one point, he asked me, "Should I just accept this and try to be the best Christian that I can?" I told him that I understood where he was coming from— that there are times when we simply don't want to seek or receive any more prayer because we are discouraged. I told him it was OK not to go for prayer at every service. Sometimes we have no expectation for healing. But when we do have expectation, we should definitely get prayer. It's so important that people not feel guilt or condemnation in the midst of their struggles.

Because of his headaches, he couldn't be in the meetings during worship, so he came with his wife and their son the second night, after the meeting was over, when we were praying for the sick. He came up to me, and he told me, "I am supposed to go to Johns Hopkins to have another surgery on my neck, a fourth fusion. I already can't look up and see the stars. I can't look down and see my shoes. I can't look to the left or to the right. All I can do is move my eyes up and down, left and right, and even when I do that, you can hear the grinding in my neck." I could hear it too. "I'm not a good father or husband anymore because of the pain," he told me. "I'm ashamed of how I treat my family sometimes, but I'm in so much pain that I can't help it. You have got to pray for me! I can't deal with another surgery! I can't stand being such an awful dad."

He was a desperate man. I knew his faith level was at rock bottom, and I had to somehow encourage him and me. "How do you know if you have faith for healing?" I asked. "I'll tell you how you know," I continued. "It's not what you believe; it's what you do. I am taking my faith that God will heal, even when I don't see it, and your faith to come one more time for healing; and I'm going to pray, because I never quit praying for the sick and believing for healing." What he didn't know was that at that moment, I didn't have faith to pray for his neck. It just wasn't there. Then suddenly I remembered the Lord awakening me that morning with a mental picture of pain that radiated down the left arm.

"Randy," I said, "do you happen to have pain going down your left arm?" He said that he did, from the pinched nerve in his neck. It was a burning pain that radiated down his arm. That seemed like a good starting point for prayer; and so, I began to pray for the pain in his arm. As I prayed, he said the pain in his left arm was diminishing. I continued to pray, and he said, "All the pain just left my arm!" With my faith level rising, I started praying for the migraine headaches, and almost immediately he said, "I feel power like electricity and heat on my head." My faith level was pretty high at that point; and so, I pressed in, and then he said, "For the first time in six years, I have no headache!" My faith level was off the charts at that point. "I command the pain in your neck to leave now," I said, "and I bless this neck in Jesus's name." With that, he jumped up and grabbed his son. His wife was crying, and I was jumping and twirling around. I didn't know it at the time, but in the Book of Hebrews, one of the words for praise is to jump and twirl. I can imagine that this word came about in response to what the ancient Church saw people do when they were healed. I started jumping and twirling too, and when I came down, a woman grabbed me and said, "Now, pray for me." And I thought, "Well I didn't even get to celebrate very long. Here is another one."

A version of this testimony can be found in Randy Clark's
The Thrill of Victory and The Agony of Defeat

Neck Pain—Frozen Neck

An elderly woman carefully made her way through the crowd toward the front where I was standing. As I raised my hand in response to what Randy was saying, I saw her fall to the floor. She was lying about five or six feet away from me, with a few people between us. My attention was taken away so I didn't go to her. Not knowing what her issues were, I decided to pray in tongues for her for about fifteen seconds. Immediately, she started to move her head and neck. About half an hour later, she came to me and said that she'd had a frozen neck for more than five years, and for the first time it was better! She'd had some sort of accident that had caused her neck issues. She said that she felt "led" to me and that when she fell down under the power of the Holy Spirit, she felt heat in her neck. When she got up, she could turn her head with no pain! I believe that the Holy Spirit, through an angel, had touched and healed her!

Bill

Pastor

Global Awakening mission trip to Mexico

Shoulder—Frozen; Lameness

I prayed for a woman whose shoulder had been frozen for twenty years. She could not raise her hand higher than her waist. I laid my hand on her shoulder and began to pray. As I prayed, I literally felt her bones shifting under my hand. She was totally healed and began raising her hand way above her head praising God! She had walked in on a crutch, and God healed her legs as well, so she walked out carrying the crutch. Praise God!

Londa

Associate Pastor

Global Awakening mission trip to Brazil

Spine—Curvature; Leg Length Discrepancy; Stomach Pain

Louise, a seventeen-year-old, came to us for prayer for curvature of her spine. Her left leg was shorter than the right one. Earlier in the day, she had also been experiencing pains and cramping in her stomach area. I started by praying for her spine, commanding it to line up and be normal. Then I rebuked the pains and cramping in her stomach while my interpreter went to get a chair for Louise to sit in. I had her sit in the chair, and then I held up her legs to check the length. The left leg was about a half-inch shorter than the right. With my eyes on her feet, I asked the Lord to grow out the shorter leg. Within just a minute, it grew out to match the right. She jumped up excited and happy. Then the Lord led me to pray prophetically for her to have boldness to testify of her healing and that as she did, she would have boldness to lead others to Jesus. She came back later beaming to tell us that she had removed the lift in her shoe and that her hips were straight and her spine healed!

Rod
Regional Distributor
Global Awakening mission trip to Curitiba, Brazil

Spine—Crooked; Crooked Wrist

The first night we were in Pemba, we did an outreach and saw God do some amazing things. We were able to pray for scores of people with some amazing results. One man came up for prayer for a crooked spine. The top of his back was about 15 percent to the left of where it should have been. I prayed a few minutes, and his back straightened about 5 percent. I was thrilled and decided not to stop. I continued to pray, and after a few minutes, his back straightened another 5 percent with a jerk. I kept praying for him, and after a couple minutes more, his back snapped completely into place. Wow!! I got to pray for another guy who had a wrist that looked as if it had been broken and not set properly. I prayed for a few minutes, and there was a pop; and the wrist was straightened. Is God awesome or what!

Daniel
Global Awakening mission trip to Mozambique

Spine—Painful Tumors

Valerie, age twenty-two, came for prayer in a power-packed meeting in Buenos Aires, Argentina. She showed us tumors on her lower spine below the belt. Two Argentines (a catcher and an interpreter) and I felt them. There were three tumors the size of an almond. We began to pray, and Valerie felt heat. The interpreter became hot, and the catcher began to feel the heat too. Valerie began to shake violently as the Spirit of God touched her. She fell forward and continued to shake. When the shaking subsided, all three of us checked the tumors again, and they had disappeared! Glory to God! Praise the name of Jesus forever! Jesus is the Healer.

Rob and Judy
Global Awakening mission trip to Argentina

Toe—Cracked Bone

A young woman came for prayer who complained of pain from a cracked bone in her foot. She is a ballerina and called to dance before the Lord. The bone connected to her big toe—the largest bone in the foot—was cracked about two inches long, beginning at the toe joint and going up toward the ankle. My interpreter and I prayed for about two minutes; then I asked her to do something she could not do because of the broken toe. She put on her ballerina slippers and did a toe stand and then declared, "I couldn't do this! There is no pain! I am healed!" Praise God!!

Danny Silk
Pastor, Bethel Church
Global Awakening mission trip to Goiânia, Brazil

Wrist—Broken; Forgiveness

I prayed for a young woman who said that six years ago she had her right wrist slammed in a bus door and it had never healed properly. It caused her much pain when she moved it and when she wrote. I could see the deformity. There was a lump on the top of her wrist from the bone. I prayed for healing, and nothing happened. I then asked her if she was angry at anyone who had been involved in the accident, and she said she was. The man who makes change on the bus had slammed the door on her wrist, and she was very angry and had not forgiven him. Every time she felt the pain in her wrist she got angry all over again. I took her wrist in my hands and told her she needed to pray to forgive the man. As she prayed, I actually felt the bones began to shift and click into place. When she ended her prayer, I took my hands away from her wrist, and she looked at it and moved her hand up and down. Then she got this look of astonishment on her face and burst into tears and began jumping up and down. She was trembling and crying because for the first time in six years she could move her wrist without any pain. The bone lump was gone too. She was healed!

Carol

Pastor

Global Awakening mission trip to Vitória, Brazil

Wrist—Broken

During ministry time, our speaker asked me to pray for a man with a broken left wrist. The bones were in correct alignment but had never grown back together after eight years. The speaker called me over to pray because he was sure he'd heard me say during my five-step teaching that I'd successfully prayed for broken bones before. I hadn't said that and told him so, but he was absolutely certain. When my translator confirmed that the word "bones" had never passed my lips, we came to believe the speaker had just heard it in the Spirit, as a word of knowledge. With that encouragement, I prayed for the man's wrist, and in a few minutes, it was 100 percent healed! He could move it in all the ways that were impossible before. When I first started praying for this man, I felt full of faith because I had some five to eight healings take place very quickly before this.

Sonja

Teacher

Global Awakening mission trip to Brazil

Wrist Pain

One night after teaching in my Baptist church, we had a time of testimony. These testimony times give people an opportunity to brag about what God has done in the past week. At one point, Sister June stood up and said, "Brother Randy, I think I'm havin' one of them there words you've been talkin' about, because my right wrist is just killin' me and there ain't anything wrong with my right wrist!" I turned and asked the congregation if there was anyone there with a problem with their right wrist, but no one responded. June sat back down thinking maybe she hadn't heard correctly. Now, I knew that Barbara, the wife of one of my best friends in the church—Tommy was his name, and he was a deacon—had undergone surgery on both wrists. The surgeon had inserted plastic pieces in her wrists, and she had been in tremendous pain ever since. She couldn't do much of anything because of the pain. But because no one responded, I was ready to move on, when Barbara stood up crying. She had actually fallen over in the pew because she was crying so hard, and that's why she hadn't responded right away. She was amazed that this word was for her. We prayed for Barbara, and her wrists were completely healed. On the way home, the pain came back, but she spoke to it and said, "I'll not receive you in Jesus's name! Leave!" The pain left again and never returned.

Told by Randy Clark in his sermon
titled "Words of Knowledge"

Wrist Pain

A woman came for prayer indicating that she had pain in her left wrist. There was no interpreter available, yet the Holy Spirit gave me the few words I needed. I examined her hand for carpel tunnel syndrome. She did not have the symptoms for that or tendonitis so I made an assumption that it was arthritis. I prayed against arthritis and gently "pulled" the pain out of her wrist through her fingertips. She was 100 percent healed. Amen!

Louise
Software Engineer

URINARY SYSTEM

The URINARY SYSTEM consists of the kidneys, ureters, and urinary bladder. It acts as a drainage system to remove urine from the body while helping to balance water and chemicals. The nephrons in the kidneys filter urea, a byproduct of food metabolism, from the blood.

But whoever drinks the water I give them will never thirst. Indeed, the water I give them will become in them a spring of water welling up to eternal life.
—JOHN 4:14

Kidney Issues; Allergies; Back Pain; Hearing Loss

Monday evening I prayed with a woman who had been healed of kidney trouble. I helped her to pray for six other people with kidney issues, and all six she prayed for were healed. I then prayed for a woman with contact allergies, and the rash on her neck instantly cleared. The miracles did not stop there. I also prayed for a man with lower back pain, and he was healed. The most exciting part for me, though, was the woman healed of kidney issues and the way the Lord used her to heal others of the same thing. One last miracle I would like to share—I prayed for the drummer on the worship team who had hearing damage caused by exposure to constant loud noise. Praise the Lord; the drummer was healed!

Bob
Physician
Global Awakening mission trip to Rio de Janeiro, Brazil

Kidney Issues

I had an opportunity to pray for a Baptist pastor who was frustrated because he couldn't hear from God. During the prayer time, I received prophetic words that were exactly what the pastor had been asking God for. I then spent a little time with him and two others, giving them a quick lesson on how to hear from God. Then, the Lord released a healing ministry over this pastor. He was able to pray for a woman with pain in her back. The Lord gave him a vision of her kidney and told him how to pray. He prayed God's prayer, and she was instantly healed. God is so good!

Norman
Global Awakening mission trip to New Zealand

Kidney Issues

During one of the outreaches, Randy had a word of knowledge for "right kidney." A man immediately in front of me raised his hand to indicate that he had that condition. I began to pray, and within just one minute, he started jumping up and down saying he was pain-free!

Dale
Pastor
Global Awakening mission trip to Mozambique

Kidney Stones

During one of the ministry times, we prayed for a man who had tremendous pain in his kidneys. He had been in the hospital the day before and was scheduled for an MRI. I prayed; the Holy Spirit came upon him strongly, and he was touched. He was hot all over and told me that he felt the Lord strongly, and it felt like God opened up his side like a zipper and went in and touched where the kidneys were and then he was totally pain-free.

Lisa
Church Janitorial Staff
Global Awakening mission trip to Brazil

Heal the sick, raise the dead, cleanse those who have leprosy,
drive out demons.
Freely you have received; freely give.
—Matthew 10:8

INDEX

A

abandonment, rejection and, 48–49

abdominal cancer, 17–18

abdominal pain, 58–50

abortion, 73–74, 77–80

Achilles tendon, 179–180

acid reflux, 85

addiction, 43, 67

adultery, 77–80

AIDS, 115–118

alcoholism, 43–44

allergies, 118, 263

aneurism, 181

ankle

    injury, 153–154, 238

    pain, 33–34, 179–180

    sprains, 139, 167–168

    twist, 162

anxiety, 44–46

arm

    length discrepancy, 64–65, 140–141, 247

    lumps, 144

    mobility issue, 162

    pain, 75–76, 140

    paralysis, 148, 162

    weak muscles, 139–140

asthma, 119–120

astigmatism, 175

B

back pain, 19–21, 46, 73–74,
    141–147, 173–176, 183–184, 199–
    200, 233–235, 248, 263

back realignment, 236–237

back, broken, 101–109

black magic, 54

blindness, 177–182, 190–191, 211

blood pressure, high, 38–39, 151–153, 244

blood sacrifices, 62–63

bone

    cancer, 27–28

    marrow transplant, 70–71

brain

    cancer, 128

    disorder, 46–47

    tumor, 17–18

breast

    cancer, 17–21, 77–80

    feeding issues, 219

    lump, 47–48

    pain, 219

    tumors, 28–29, 220

breathing issues, 225

C

calf injury, 238

cancer, 15, 21–22

carpal tunnel syndrome, 182

cataracts, 182–184

chest

    pain, 33, 55–56

    tumor, 22–23

child abuse, 50, 69–70

child birth issues, 173–175

circulatory system, 31

collar bone, loss of mobility, 147–148

concussion, 101–109

confusion, 44–46

congestive heart failure, 34–36

cripple, 148–150

Crohn's Disease, 86–87

crossed eyes, 72, 184

D

deafness, 54–55, 184–195.
    See also hearing loss
    -muteness and, 201–202

degenerative neurological disease, 63–64

deliverance, 41

dental issues, 87–89

depression, 55

diabetes, 99, 179–180
foot infection, 99–100

digestive disorders, 89–91

digestive system, 83

digestive upset, 225

divine stories of healing. *See also* Global Awakening mission; Global Awakening Youth Power Invasion
cancer, 15–29
circulatory system, 31–39
deliverance, 41–82
digestive system, 83–96
endocrine system, 97–111
immune system, 113–123
integumentary system, 125–129
marriage and family issues, 131–135
muscular system, 137–169
nervous system, 171–215
reproductive system, 217–221
respiratory system, 223–230
skeletal system, 231–260
urinary system, 261–269

dizziness, 225

drugs, 49–50

dyslexia, 196

E

ear
bleeding, 176–177
infection, 192–193
missing, 196
pain, 165, 197

eczema, 127–128

emotional healing, 44, 74

emotional pain, 73

emotional wounding, 144, 176

emotions, damaged, 53–54

endocrine system, 97

endometriosis, 220

epilepsy, 101–109

equilibrium issues, 161

eye. *See also* vision
cloudiness, 51
glass, 198–199
issues, 206
pressure, 55–56

F

fallopian tube tumor, 23

family, 131

fear, 56–57

femur bone injury, 246

fever, high, 93–94

fibromyalgia, 197–198

fingers
broken, 241
pain, 155

flu symptoms, 225

foot/feet
arthritis, 233
broken, 239–240
calcium deposits and pain, 154–155
infection, 99–100
injury, 153–54
loss of sensation, 48–49
multiple surgeries, 239
pain, 179–180

forehead
lumps, 241–242

G

gallstones, 91

generational curses of infirmity, 47–48

generational sin, 57–58

genetic illness, 70–71

glaucoma, 198

Global Awakening mission
in Argentina, 46, 143, 176, 207, 221, 235, 257
in Australia, 148, 168–169, 173, 244
in Brazil, 19–21, 23, 25, 28–29, 37, 39, 44, 49, 51, 54–56, 60–62, 64–68, 72, 75–77, 85, 88, 91, 93–96, 115, 121–122,

127–128, 139–40, 142–144, 147, 150, 153, 155, 158, 161–164, 167, 177, 179–181, 195, 200–206, 211, 213, 215, 220–221, 225–227, 229–230, 234, 237, 239–240, 243–245, 243–246, 248, 251, 255–256

in China, 38, 61, 89, 175, 182–190, 192, 238, 249, 251, 257–258, 263–64

in Colombia, 50, 198, 230, 238

in Cuba, 27, 123

in England, 241

in Europe, 73

in India, 95, 121, 148, 160, 166, 182, 191, 194, 242

in Mexico, 33, 99–100, 118, 196–197, 255

in Middle East, 59, 135, 165

in Mozambique, 141, 158, 165, 219, 242, 256, 264

in New Zealand, 47, 74, 144, 154, 166, 233, 263

in Spain, 75, 241

in Switzerland, 241

in Ukraine, 22, 43, 50, 57, 74, 77, 101, 129, 155, 219

Global Awakening Youth Power Invasion
in Brazil, 18, 23, 34, 43, 48, 55, 93, 128, 141, 160, 164, 180, 182, 184, 192, 193, 198, 199, 206, 220, 226, 239, 247

guilt and shame, 73–74

H

hands
arthritis, 115, 183
cyst, 127
loss of sensation, 48–49
lumps, 127
paralysis, 148

head
ache, 58–60, 181, 190–191, 242
injury, 241–243
tumor, 221

healing stories. *See* divine stories of healing

hearing loss, 48–49, 183–184, 199–200, 263. *See also* deafness

heart problems, 37–38

heel, pain, 155

hemorrhoids, 89–91

hip
alignment issues, 244
bone spur, 237
pain, 33–34, 243
smashed bone, 243–244

I

idolatry, 51

immune system, 113

infertility, 60, 221

insomnia, 68–69

integumentary system, 125

intestinal issues, 211

intestinal problems, 60–61

intimacy, 12–14

irritable bowel syndrome, 91–93

J

jaw
broken, 85–86
pain, 89

joint pain, 67, 121, 127

K

kidney
issues, 263–264
stones, 264

knee
dry socket, 244–245
pain, 22–23, 33–34, 159–60, 183–184, 197–198, 242, 245
surgical implantation, 245
torn meniscus, 156–157
weak muscles, 158
withered muscles, 157–58

L

labyrinthitis/balance Issues, 201

lameness, 61, 63–66, 99, 161–164, 194–195, 245, 255

leg
broken, 246

calf muscle injury, 164–165
circulation issues, 33–34
crooked, 249–251
hamstring torn, 168
length discrepancy, 64–65, 76–77, 164,
    244, 247–251, 255–256
pain, 155, 202
surgically implanted, 251
legal precedents, 2
ligaments
torn, 168–169
liver pain, 93
lung cancer, 24–25
lung infection, 225–226
lying, 53–54
spirit, 56–57

M

macumba, 54, 62–66
marital problems, 133–135
marriage, 131
meningitis, 201–202
migraine, 251–254
ministering
healing and, 12–14
mitral valve prolapse, 156–157
mouth, rashes, 93–94
multifocal leukoencephalopathy,
    progressive, 115–117
murder, 73–74
muscle deterioration, 167
muscular system, 137
muteness, 186–187, 193–195

N

nails, ingrown, 128
neck
frozen, 254–255
injury, 251–254
lump, 62
nodes, 66–67
pain, 165–166, 202, 254–255
nervous system, 171

O

obedience, 12–14
occult, 47–48, 68
osteoporosis, 67
ovarian cyst, 221
ovarian problems, 77

P

pancoast tumor, 24–25
pancreatic cancer, 25–26
paralysis, 49–50, 65, 203–206
Parkinson's disease, 68, 100–11
Pepto-Bismol miracle, 59
perversion, 48–49
polio, 120–121
post-traumatic stress disorder
    (PTSD), 68–70
prostitution, 57–58, 62–63

R

religious spirit, 76–77
reproductive system, 217
respiratory system, 223
rheumatic fever, 121
rheumatoid arthritis, 121–122
ritual abuse, 70–71

S

satanism, 55–56, 59–60
sciatic nerve pain, 176
scoliosis, 71–72
scratchy throat, 225
seizures, 101–109
self-hate, 128–129
sense loss, smelling, 226
sexual abuse, 77–80
sexual sin, 46–47, 53–54, 57–58, 62–63, 73
shingles, 122–123
shoulder
frozen, 255
injury, 166
issues, 77–80
pain, 144, 166–167, 176

sinus condition, 227
Sjögren's syndrome, 122
skeletal system, 231
skin blotches, 128–129
skull malformation, 72
sleep apnea, 227–229
soul ties, 60, 73
speech impediment, 207–209
spina bifida, 209–211
spine
    alignment issues, 244
    crooked, 256
    curvature, 255–256
    damage from anesthesia, 175
    dislocation, 233–234
    herniated disks, 61, 145–147
    injury, 205–206, 211–213
    tumor, 213, 256–257
spirit of death, 48–50, 56–57, 73–74.
    See also abortion; suicide
spirit of rejection, 75–76
spiritism, 54–56, 76–77
stomach
    cancers, 26–28
    pain, 85, 99, 255–256
    tumors, 94–95
strokes, 39, 65–66
suicide, 51–53, 76–77

T

tendons, torn, 168–69
testimony
    faith on, 9–10
    glory of God and, 11–12
    prophetic revelation and, 10–11
Thrill of Victory, The (Clark),
    18, 26, 111, 213, 254
throat
    dry, 95–96
    lumps, 95
thyroid disorder, 55–56
tibia bone injury, 246
tinnitus, 195

toes
    cracked bone, 257
    pain, 151–53, 215
tooth pain, 89
tuberculosis, 229

U

ulcer, 95–96
unemployment, 155
urinary system, 261
uterine problems, 20–21, 77
uterine tumors, 28–29

V

vision. *See also* eye
    deterioration, 215
    loss, 48–49, 67
    tunnel, 214
vocal cords
    damages, 229–230

W

white magic, 54
witchcraft, 46–47, 51, 55–55,
    57–60, 69–70, 77–82
word curse, 46
World Health Organization, on cancer, 15
wounds, bullet, 48–50
wrist
    broken, 145–147, 257–258
    crooked, 256
    cyst, 127
    pain, 259–260
    sore, 167–68

About Randy Clark

Randy Clark, with a D.Min. from United Theological Seminary, is the founder of Global Awakening, a teaching, healing, and impartation ministry that crosses denominational lines. An in-demand international speaker, he leads the Apostolic Network of Global Awakening and travels extensively for conferences, international missions, leadership training, and humanitarian aid. Randy and his wife, DeAnne, live in Pennsylvania.